NATIONAL AUDUBON SOCIETY®

FIRST
FIELD
GUIDE
NIGHT SKY

NATIONAL AUDUBON SOCIETY®

FIRST FIELD GUIDE

NIGHT SKY

Written by
Gary Mechler

Sky maps by
Wil Tirion

Scholastic Inc.

New York   Toronto   London   Auckland   Sydney
Mexico City   New Delhi   Hong Kong

The National Audubon Society, established in 1905, has 550,000 members and more than 500 chapters nationwide. Its mission is to conserve and restore natural ecosystems, focusing on wildlife and plant life, and these guides are part of that mission. Celebrating the beauty and wonders of nature, Audubon looks toward its second century of educating people of all ages. For information about Audubon membership, contact:

National Audubon Society
700 Broadway
New York, NY 10003-9562
800-274-4201

http://www.audubon.org/

Copyright © 1999 by Chanticleer Press, Inc.
All rights reserved. Published by Scholastic Inc.
SCHOLASTIC and associated logos are trademarks and/or registered trademarks of Scholastic Inc.

LIBRARY OF CONGRESS CATALOGING-IN-PUBLICATION DATA

Mechler, Gary.
    National Audubon Society first field guide. Night sky/ by Gary Mechler.
        p.   cm.
    Includes bibliographical references and index.
    Summary: A field guide to the night sky, explaining through text and maps how to locate and identify stars, planets, meteors, comets, and constellations.
        ISBN 0-590-64085-2 (hc) — ISBN 0-590-64086-0 (pb)
        1. Astronomy—Juvenile literature. 2. Astronomy—Observers' manuals—Juvenile literature. National Audubon Society—Handbooks, manuals, etc.—Juvenile literature. [1. Astronomy—Observers' manuals.] I. Title. II. Title: Night sky.
QB46.M495 1999
520—dc21   98-51876   CIP   AC

10 9 8 7 6 5 4 3 2 1   9/9 0/0 01 02 03

Printed in Hong Kong
First printing, August 1999
Front cover photograph: Comet Hyakutake by Jerry Schad/Science Source/Photo Researchers, Inc.
National Audubon Society® is a registered trademark of National Audubon Society, Inc., all rights reserved.

Contents

About this book

Whether you are watching the moon rise, awaiting a solar eclipse, or looking for constellation shapes in the stars, this book will help you to look at the night sky the way an astronomer does. The book is divided into four parts:

Spiral galaxy M83 in the constellation Hydra

PART 1: What is astronomy?

tells you about astronomy—the study of outer space—and the things astronomers have learned over the years about the sun, Earth and the other planets, the stars, and the universe.

PART 2: How to look at the sky

gives you the information you need to begin identifying constellations, stars, and planets, and to look at the moon, eclipses, comets, meteor showers, and other wonderful things in the sky.

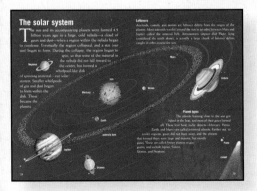

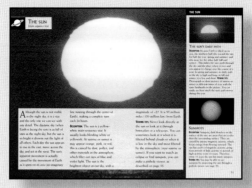

PART 3: The field guide includes detailed descriptions, sky maps, and photographs of things that you can see in the sky, including the moon, planets, and comets of our solar system, and the stars and constellations of our own galaxy and beyond.

PART 4: The reference section at the back of the book includes a helpful glossary of terms used by astronomers; lists of useful books, CDs, Web sites, and organizations; tables giving dates and locations of planets, eclipses, and meteor showers; and an index of the planets, moons, stars, constellations, and other objects that are covered in the guide.

What is an astronomer?

An astronomer is a scientist who studies outer space and everything in it. But you don't have to be a scientist to study space. You don't even need a telescope. The sky is there for all to see, to study, to wonder about, and to learn from. Because the subject is so vast (it's the universe!), you are bound to find something that will intrigue you and challenge you to learn more.

Rooftop astronomy

Maria Mitchell (1818–1889) was born on Nantucket, an island off the coast of Massachusetts. Mitchell became interested in astronomy when she was young, studying the sky from her rooftop. In 1847 she became the first astronomer to discover a comet while using a telescope. Mitchell taught science and astronomy to young women for 23 years at Vassar College, where she was the nation's first female astronomy professor and observatory director.

YOU CAN BE AN ASTRONOMER, TOO!
Do you like to look at the moon and the stars? Are you curious about the things you see? Do you try to find out more about them? If you answer "yes" to these questions, then you have the mind of an astronomer.

A sky-watcher's tools
When you go out to look at the sky, bring your field guide, a flashlight, binoculars (if you have them), and paper and pencils for taking notes. Fasten a red filter or a piece of red cellophane or cloth over your flashlight. If you want to get a telescope, try to find one with a large "aperture" number; the greater the aperture, the bigger the lens opening, which means the telescope gathers more light and you can see more.

Sky-watching tips

- Look at your field guide before you go out and plan what you want to see. Mark the pages you will need with bookmarks.

- Wear more layers of clothing than you think you will need, and bring a blanket, sleeping bag, or lawn chair to sit or lie on.

- Use the red light from your flashlight to look at your field guide once your eyes are used to the dark. If you turn on a bright light to look at your book, you will have to wait for your eyes to adjust again.

- If you are using binoculars, be sure to find a firm place to rest your elbows to keep the binoculars still.

- Always go out at night with an adult.

What is astronomy?

Astronomy is the study of everything beyond Earth and how it came to be: stars, planets, moons, comets, asteroids, dust, gases, nebulas, galaxies, and the universe itself.

Astronomy vs astrology

Early people learned the patterns of stars and followed the paths of planets across the sky. These were the beginnings of both astronomy, the science, and astrology, the belief that the stars and planets influenced people's lives and events on Earth.

What's the time?

How did people tell time before they had clocks? By studying the motions of Earth in space. The rotation (spinning) of Earth gives us our daily sunrise and sunset and our 24-hour day. Earth's revolution around the sun in its orbit defines the year. The month is based upon the time needed for the moon to orbit Earth. The seven days of the week are named for the sun, the moon, and the five easily visible planets.

People from different parts of the ancient world built large structures that were used for time-keeping, ceremonies, and sky-observing. One of those structures was Stonehenge (pictured here), built around 2800 B.C. in England—and still standing! Ancient travelers learned to use the sun, moon, and stars to help them find their way on land and sea. Sailors, for example, used the North Star, Polaris, to tell directions.

Astronomy today

People learned more about the nature of the universe in the 20th century than in all the previous centuries of humanity combined. Astronomers discovered galaxies and learned that we live within one (the Milky Way, a spiral galaxy). They also learned that the universe had a distinct origin, called "the Big Bang," and figured out how stars and planets are made and how old many of them are. But even though so much has been learned, there is enough out there to keep astronomers busy for centuries into the future.

Modern-day astronomers have learned that there are tens of billions of galaxies in the universe, each with billions of stars—and probably many planets as well. The Whirlpool (above) is a spiral galaxy with a smaller galaxy near it located in the constellation Canes Venatici.

The science of astronomy

Astronomy is the oldest science. Prehistoric people around the world studied the night sky, but the ancient Greeks (600 B.C. to A.D. 400) first developed the science of astronomy. They set aside the age-old notion that nature was ruled by supernatural forces beyond our understanding, in favor of the notion that nature was explainable. With this new way of thinking, they were able to begin understanding some of the mysteries of space.

It's all Greek

Greek thinkers tested their ideas, laid the groundwork for modern science, and developed mathematics. They were able to prove that Earth is round and even measured its size. But they didn't get everything right: Most believed that Earth sat unmoving at the center of the entire universe, with everything else orbiting around it.

Astronomers study space from observatories—centers with large telescopes and other astronomical equipment. Most observatories, including Kitt Peak National Observatory near Tucson, Arizona (pictured here), are built on mountaintops or in desert areas, where skies tend to be clear and dry.

Scientific revolution

In 1543 a Polish scientist named Nicolaus Copernicus (1473–1543) proposed a daring idea: that the sun—not Earth—was at the center of the universe. Building on this idea, later scientists, including Galileo Galilei (1564–1642) of Italy,

Galileo demonstrating his telescope in Venice, Italy, 1609

developed theories about the motions of the sun and planets that still stand. English scientist Isaac Newton (1642–1700) furthered our understanding of how things move in the universe. He formulated a clear notion of force, in general, and the gravity force, in particular. To do all that, he invented a type of mathematics called calculus.

INTO THE FUTURE

Galileo was the first person to turn a telescope toward the sky. As equipment improved over the years, new discoveries came. Thanks to the work of people who lived hundreds of years ago, modern-day astronomers have been able to learn how stars and planets are made, study the origins of the universe, and even travel in space.

The Hubble Space Telescope, in orbit 360 miles (575 km) above Earth, takes pictures of the space around us.

The universe

When you look up at the sky, day or night, you are looking out into the universe. The universe is so vast you can see only a very tiny bit of it. Astronomers think the universe is about 14 billion years old.

You are here

What do you see?
All the stars you can see in the night sky are in our home galaxy, the Milky Way. Earth is located out toward the edge of our disk-shaped galaxy. In the summer, we look toward the nucleus, or center, of the galaxy. The light from many billions of stars blends together to create the milky streak of light that we see then. At other times of the year we face away from the center and can't see the star clouds of the Milky Way at all.

WHAT'S OUT THERE?
We can see just a tiny portion of the universe when we gaze at the night sky: the moon, a few thousand nearby stars, some of the planets, a galaxy or two. What we can't see are billions and billions more stars that make up the Milky Way. Other stars form other galaxies. Large clouds of gas and dust swirl around and among many stars. Galaxies are grouped in clusters, and these clusters are grouped in superclusters. What's in between all those things? Nothing but cold, airless, noiseless space.

THE SPEED OF LIGHT

The stars you see in the night sky are typically many trillions of miles away. Astronomers measure such huge distances in "light-years." One light-year is the distance light travels in a year's time. Traveling at about 186,000 miles per second (300,000 km/sec), light covers 5,900,000,000,000 miles (9,500,000,000,000 km) in one year. Sirius, the brightest star in the night sky, is 8.8 light-years, or 50,800,000,000,000 miles (83,600,000,000,000 km) from Earth. If you could travel to Sirius at the speed of light, it would take nearly nine years to get there! If you traveled at 55 miles per hour (90 km/hr), the speed limit on many highways, how long would it take? More than 100 million years!

Nucleus

MILKY WAY GALAXY

Looking back in time

Our universe is big in time as well as space. Stars in our galaxy are thousands of light-years away. Other galaxies are millions of light-years away. When astronomers study these faraway objects (with very powerful telescopes) they are actually looking back in time! The light from these distant stars takes thousands to millions of years to reach us.

This Hubble Space Telescope image shows dozens of galaxies that are 10 to 12 billion light-years from Earth. We see them as they looked 10 to 12 billion years ago!

15

Galaxies

Galaxies are large groups of stars and other material (mainly gas and dust). There are several different types of galaxies, and they come in all sizes. Our Milky Way is a spiral galaxy about 80,000 light-years across with about 200 billion stars.

ELLIPTICAL GALAXIES

Elliptical galaxies have the shape of a sphere or a somewhat flattened sphere. Most galaxies in the universe are elliptical.

Elliptical galaxy M87, in the constellation Virgo

How big?

The smallest galaxies, called dwarf galaxies, have several million stars and may measure 5,000 light-years across. The largest galaxies, the giant ellipticals, have several trillion stars and are about 300,000 light-years across.

SPIRAL GALAXIES

Many galaxies, including the Milky Way, are flattened spiral-shaped disks. They have a bulge at the center called the nucleus. Stars and clouds of glowing gas and dust (nebulas) compose the swirling pattern of the surrounding disk.

The Sombrero Galaxy, in the constellation Virgo, is a spiral galaxy. We view it from the side and see the plane of the disk as a dark line. The nucleus shines brightly in the center, and gas and dust clouds glow above and below.

IRREGULAR AND PECULIAR GALAXIES

Many galaxies don't have the clear shape of a ball or a disk. Some of these are small and are called irregular galaxies. Others, called peculiar galaxies, are usually powerfully energetic because they are actually two galaxies colliding. Such collisions generate a lot of energy.

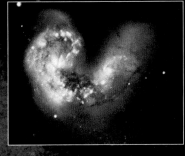

The Antennae, two galaxies that are crashing into each other in the constellation Corvus, are called peculiar galaxies.

This spiral galaxy, found in the constellation Virgo, is called M100. It belongs to a cluster of galaxies called the Virgo Cluster. The "M" stands for Charles Messier (1730–1817), a French astronomer who discovered many objects in the sky and printed them in a list called the Messier Catalog.

QUASARS AND BLACK HOLES

The most powerful galaxies are the distant quasars. They can be detected by the energy flowing from their centers, at which lie supermassive black holes with a lot of matter spiraling into them. Energy is released by this infalling matter. Because quasars and the other most distant galaxies are so far away, light from them has taken most of the lifetime of the universe to reach us. When astronomers look at them they get a glimpse of the early universe!

17

Nebulas

In interstellar ("between the stars") space, atoms and molecules of gas and dust form huge clouds called nebulas (or nebulae, pronounced NEB-you-lee). Stars and planets are born in nebulas.

SPACE DUST BALLS

Dust in space gathers in much the same way as dust in your house. Air currents in your home carry dust. The dust settles out where the currents weaken, forming dust balls. In outer space, instead of air currents, gravitational and magnetic fields sweep gases and dust grains together—but it takes tens of millions of years for the gaseous dust balls (nebulas) to form.

Planets forming in rotating disk

Star forming at center

STAR CLUSTERS

Stars are born in clusters. There are two basic types of star clusters: open clusters, which are loose collections of stars that were born at about the same time (such as the Pleiades), and globular clusters, which are massive sphere-shaped clumps of stars. Open clusters are usually relatively young stars; globular clusters are older stars.

A star is born

The star-making process begins when a region within a nebula becomes so compressed from the nebula's internal motions that gravity takes over and forces it to collapse into a compressed, rotating flattened disk. If the region at the center of the disk is compressed enough, over time it begins to burn energy (through nuclear fusion) and is then called a star.

Planets from dust

Planets are usually born along with a star. They form within the rotating, flattened disk surrounding the star when whirlpools form in the gas and dust. As the material in the disk rotates, dust gathers in the whirlpools and begins clumping together. These clumps eventually become planets. Our flat, rotating solar system was formed from a disk of compressed matter in a nebula about 4.5 billion years ago.

A star dies

Some nebulas are formed as stars die. Some stars die with something like a last sigh, puffing out a spherical shell of gas, called a planetary nebula. Other stars go out with a bang, ending in a violent explosion and blasting out gas in all directions. These exploding stars are called supernovas, and the resulting nebulas are supernova remnants.

BIRTH OF A SOLAR SYSTEM IN A NEBULA

What is a star?

Stars are large balls of hot, shining, electrically charged gases, called plasma. The gases are mostly hydrogen and helium, but there are other elements as well. Stars come in a wide range of sizes, temperatures, brightnesses, and even colors.

The closest star to Earth is the sun.

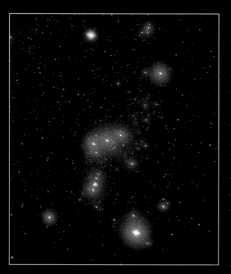

The constellation Orion, the Hunter, visible in the winter evening sky in the Northern Hemisphere, has two colorful stars. One of Orion's shoulders (the upper left corner of the figure) is marked with the red supergiant star Betelgeuse. Diagonally below, in the Hunter's knee, is the blue giant star Rigel. For more on Orion, see pages 138–143.

Hot and cool

A star's color comes from its temperature. Blue stars are the hottest, up to 64,000° Fahrenheit (35,000° Celsius), and red stars are the coolest, at about 4,000°F (2,200°C). In between are (from hotter to cooler) white, yellow, and orange stars. Our sun, a yellow-white star, has a surface temperature of about 10,000°F (5,500°C). Typically, blue stars are hot young stars quickly burning their fuel. Red stars are longer-lived. The large ones are nearing the end of their lifetimes. Most stars in the sky aren't bright enough for the human eye to detect their colors.

This picture looks toward the center of the Milky Way, where stars and nebulas are so dense they appear as a glowing band across the summer sky.

Star light, star bright

The measure of a star's brightness in the night sky is called its apparent magnitude. The scale of star magnitudes was invented by a scientist named Hipparchus around 140 B.C. Bright stars are 1st magnitude. The faintest that can be seen with the naked eye (that means without telescopes or binoculars) are 6th magnitude. The very brightest stars and planets are brighter than 1st magnitude, so their magnitudes are in negative numbers.

Double stars

Single stars like our sun are in the minority in the universe. Though stars may look single in the night sky, close-up studies have shown that 60 to 70 percent of stars are paired with other stars. These are called double stars. There are also triple stars and double-double stars (two pairs).

Giants and dwarfs

Stars range in size from about 7,000 miles (11,000 km) in diameter (smaller than Earth, which has a diameter of about 8,000 miles, or 13,000 km) to about 900 million miles (1.5 billion km) in diameter, or 110,000 Earth diameters. The very largest stars are also the brightest. The largest and brightest are called supergiants; giants are smaller and less bright. The smallest stars are called dwarfs. Our sun is of medium size (865,000 miles, or 1.4 million km, in diameter) and brightness.

The life of a star

A star's lifetime is the period in which it actively generates energy. Stars do not remain the same throughout their lifetimes. They go through stages that last millions, sometimes even billions, of years. The longest, most stable period of a star's total lifetime (about 90 percent) is called the "main sequence" phase. During this phase hydrogen, the most abundant element, is fused into helium in the star's core.

LIFE OF A SUPER STAR

MAIN SEQUENCE
Very massive, luminous stars are many times larger, hotter, and brighter than our sun. But like ordinary stars, these super-size stars spend most of their life cycle in the main sequence, turning hydrogen in their cores into energy by nuclear fusion.

LIFE OF AN AVERAGE STAR

MAIN SEQUENCE
An average star, like our sun, spends most of its life in the main sequence phase, generating energy by nuclear fusion. Our sun has been a main sequence star for about 4.5 billion years. It will be in this phase for another 4.5 to 5 billion years before using up the store of hydrogen in its core.

RED GIANT
After the main sequence phase, a star increases its energy flow as it changes energy sources in its interior. This stronger energy flow pushes the star outward, and the star expands—sometimes to more than 100 times its original size. The star's larger, cooler surface is orange-red, and the star is called a red giant.

NEBULA
Eventually a red giant begins to run out of fuel, and the star changes again. The star itself begins to shrink and as it does it gives off a puff of gas. The gas then surrounds the star like a shell; the gas shell is called a planetary nebula.

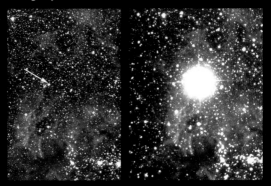

RED SUPERGIANT

A massive star turns into a huge red supergiant after the main sequence phase. A red supergiant, if placed where our sun is, would extend out beyond the orbit of Mars. There are not many of these terrifically bright stars. Antares (constellation Scorpius) and Betelgeuse (Orion) are two.

SUPERNOVA

After expanding to become a supergiant, the star has used up all its nuclear fuel. Gravity pulling inward is now stronger than nuclear reactions pushing out. The star collapses to its core and then explodes out in all directions. So much energy is released that a single supernova can outshine an entire galaxy of stars.

BLACK HOLE AND PULSAR

After a supernova explosion, what's left of the original star might shrink down to a sphere only about 10 miles (16 km) across called a neutron star or pulsar. In some cases the star may shrink to only a few miles across and become a black hole, where gravity is so strong that not even light can escape.

WHITE DWARF

After the red giant phase the star shrinks from its enormous size (perhaps as large as Earth's orbit) to about the size of Earth. The shrinking of all that material from the giant star into this compact package causes it to heat up again, so it glows white hot. It is called a white dwarf.

FAST AND FLASHY VERSUS SLOW AND DIM

Massive, highly luminous stars go through their fuel faster and live shorter lives. While stars like our sun live about 10 billion years, the really massive stars live only a few million years. Small, cool, dim stars called red dwarfs can generate their relatively meager energy for well over 100 billion years! Massive stars, such as this one shown before and after exploding as a supernova, live fast and die young.

Constellations

Constellations are imaginary games of "connect-the-dots" played on the night sky. People around the world named constellations according to the patterns they traced in the stars. Today there are 88 constellations. It is fun to try to pick out the constellations, but some require a lot of imagination to see!

A line of stars in the summer night sky (left) becomes Scorpius, the Scorpion, with a bit of imagination (right).
For more on Scorpius see pages 104–107.

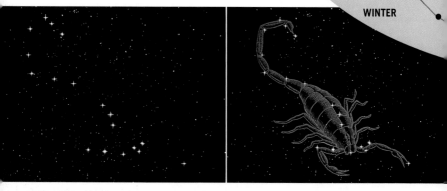

FALL

Pisces

Aries

Ecliptic

Taurus

WINTER

Why did people make constellations?

People picked out patterns in the stars to map the sky. They could then follow the motions of the stars to measure time and to find their way when traveling. Ancient Egyptian people used the star Sirius (in the constellation Canis Major) as a seasonal marker. When Sirius rose at dawn each summer the Nile River would flood the surrounding valley. Sailors used the pointer stars of the Big Dipper to find the North Star so they could keep their ships sailing in the right direction.

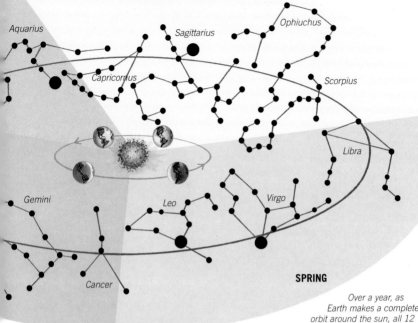

SUMMER

Aquarius

Sagittarius

Ophiuchus

Capricornus

Scorpius

Libra

Gemini

Leo

Virgo

Cancer

SPRING

CONSTELLATIONS OF THE ZODIAC

The zodiac is a band of constellations lying in the same plane as the path of Earth's orbit around the sun. This path is called the ecliptic. The planets and the sun also travel along or near this path. Think of Earth's orbit as a Frisbee, with Earth at the Frisbee's rim. The zodiac constellations are the constellations that lie even with the rim. In each season, as Earth moves in its yearly orbit, we face a different set of these constellations at night. In the day, we face the sun, and the sun lies between us and the zodiac constellations behind it. We say that the sun is "in" the constellation it is directly in front of. The superior planets, from Mars outward, are between Earth and the zodiac, so they always appear to pass in front of these constellations as well.

Over a year, as Earth makes a complete orbit around the sun, all 12 constellations of the zodiac appear in the night sky. This illustration shows which of the zodiac constellations Earth faces in each season. The constellation Ophiuchus, which is not designated a zodiac constellation, is also included because it falls within the zodiac's band. The constellations are drawn as we view them from Earth. When a planet is in a constellation that Earth faces at night, we can see it. In winter, for example, we can see a planet that is in Gemini, but not a planet that is in Scorpius, which is behind the sun and thus blocked from view.

Mythology in the sky

Ancient civilizations the world over traced patterns in the stars and attached myths and legends to the star groups. They also told stories about the planets wandering through the sky.

FIRE-BREATHING HIPPO?

The constellation Draco represented a fire-breathing dragon winding through the sky in many legends. To the Greeks it was the dragon that Hercules had to defeat in order to get the Golden Apples. But these same stars were said to be a crocodile in India and a hippopotamus in ancient Egypt.

THE MAN IN THE SKY

The constellation Orion sparkles brightly in the winter sky and is visible from all over the world. Greeks, Romans, Babylonians, Egyptians, Arabs, and other ancient people saw the figure of a man (or a god) in these stars. But Orion is an exception— most star patterns were seen as different things in different civilizations.

BEAR TALES

Ursa Major, the
Great Bear, is a
constellation with
many different stories. Several civilizations saw a bear in
these stars. In ancient Greek and Roman mythology, the
bear's tail (the three handle stars of the dipper) got
stretched out when the king of the gods, Jupiter (or
Zeus), took the bear by its tail and swung it around and
up into the sky, where it continues to whirl around the
north pole today. To North American Indians, these three
trailing stars were hunters, forever chasing the bear
around the pole.

THE FRIENDLY DOLPHIN

It is easy to see a dolphin in
the constellation Delphinus.
Dolphins were said to have
been the friends of Poseidon,
the sea god. One of Poseidon's
dolphins rescued a Greek poet and harp player, named
Arion, from being killed by a group of sailors. Apollo, the god
of poetry and music, placed the dolphin in the sky in gratitude.

The solar system

The sun and its accompanying planets were formed 4.5 billion years ago in a large, cold nebula—a cloud of gases and dust—when a region within the nebula began to condense. Eventually the region collapsed, and a star (our sun) began to form. During the collapse, the region began to spin, so that some of the material in the nebula did not fall inward to the center, but formed a whirlpool-like disk of spinning material—our solar system. Smaller whirlpools of gas and dust began to form within the disk. These became the planets.

Neptune

sun

Mercury

Earth

asteroid belt

Jupiter

Uranus

Leftovers

Asteroids, comets, and moons are leftover debris from the origin of the planets. Most asteroids revolve around the sun in an orbit between Mars and Jupiter called the asteroid belt. Astronomers suspect that Pluto, long considered the ninth planet, is actually a large chunk of leftover debris caught in orbit around the sun.

Mars

Saturn

Venus

Planet types

The planets forming close to the sun got baked in the heat, and most of their gases burned off. These four hard, rocky objects—Mercury, Venus, Earth, and Mars—are called terrestrial planets. Farther out, in cooler regions, gases did not burn away, and the planets that formed there were large and massive, but mostly gases. These are called Jovian planets or gas giants, and include Jupiter, Saturn, Uranus, and Neptune.

Pluto

comet

The sun

Our sun is a star, which means it is a hot sphere of electrically charged gases (plasma). It is a yellow-white star, average in size, in the main sequence phase of its life cycle. It lies about 93 million miles (150 million km) away, and its light takes about eight minutes to reach Earth.

WHAT IS THE SUN MADE OF?

The sun is made up of gases: It is about 92 percent hydrogen and 7 percent helium; 90 other elements, including carbon, oxygen, iron, and neon, make up the remaining 1 percent. The sun generates the energy that makes it burn (and heats up Earth) by turning hydrogen into helium. This is called nuclear fusion, and it releases a huge amount of energy.

THE SUN'S LIFETIME

Our sun is about halfway through its total lifetime. It has been in the main sequence phase of its life for about 4.5 billion years, creating energy by fusing hydrogen into helium at its core. After this phase the sun's outer atmosphere will expand and cool, and it will turn into a red giant type of star. It could grow so big that it might envelop Mercury, Venus, and Earth. That's a problem our descendants will have to deal with about 5 billion years from now.

X-ray image of the sun showing white-hot spots on the surface as well as cooler regions

CORE
The hottest part of the sun, at 27,000,000°F (15,000,000°C). Nuclear fusion occurs here.

ENVELOPE
The layer that wraps around the core. Its function is to move the energy produced in the core outward. It has two layers, an inner and an outer, which move the energy in different ways.

CORONA
The outer layer of the sun's atmosphere. Extends about 1 million miles (1,600,000 km) into space. Temperature: up to 6,300,000°F (3,500,000°C).

CHROMOSPHERE
The layer of the sun's atmosphere just above the photosphere. Temperature: 10,000–1,800,000°F (5,500–1,000,000°C).

SOLAR FLARES AND PROMINENCES
Eruptions of energy from the sun's surface. Charged particles from flares can travel as far as Earth and beyond.

SUNSPOTS
Areas of cooler temperature on the photosphere. They appear as dark spots on the sun's surface.

PHOTOSPHERE
The sun's surface and the part that shines brightly. Temperature: about 10,000°F (5,500°C).

With a diameter of 865,000 miles (1.4 million km), the sun dwarfs every planet in the solar system. It is 109 times larger than Earth and 9.7 times larger than the largest planet, Jupiter.

Mercury Venus Earth Mars Jupiter Saturn Uranus Neptune Pluto

sun

Earth and the moon

One of the four small, rocky terrestrial planets, Earth is distinctive even among its own kind. Unlike Mercury, Venus, or Mars, it has large bodies of liquid water on its surface. It has a large satellite, the moon. It is the largest and most massive of the terrestrial planets, slightly outdoing Venus. And it is the only known planet that supports life.

Earth, photographed from Apollo 17 spacecraft

Phases of the moon
Just as Earth orbits the sun, the moon orbits Earth. The constantly shifting alignment of Earth, the moon, and the sun brings about the phases of the moon as well as lunar and solar eclipses.

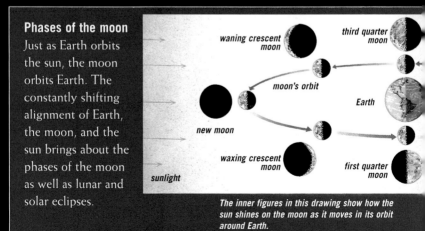

waning crescent moon

third quarter moon

moon's orbit

Earth

new moon

waxing crescent moon

first quarter moon

sunlight

The inner figures in this drawing show how the sun shines on the moon as it moves in its orbit around Earth.

INNER EARTH

At Earth's center is a metallic core of mostly iron and nickel. The core extends about halfway out to the surface. The outer part of the core is liquid and is the source of Earth's magnetic field. Surrounding the core is a rocky, metallic mantle, and around that is a thin outer crust. Volcanoes, earthquakes, and movement of the crust called continental drift have changed Earth's surface over the 4.5 billion years since it formed.

Full moon

SMASHING PLANETS

Earth's satellite, the moon, was formed in a spectacular collision of the very early Earth with a smaller planet. The collision blasted rocky debris into orbit around Earth. Over time, the debris gathered together, forming the moon. The moon is heavier on one side. The extra pull of Earth's gravity on the heavy side slowed the moon's rotation. Now the heavier side always faces Earth.

WHAT IS THE MOON MADE OF?

Like Earth, the moon has a core, mantle, and crust. The moon is nearly all rock. Its surface is full of craters, where rocks crashed into it in the early life of the solar system. Because the moon has essentially no atmosphere—and thus has no wind, rain, weathering, or erosion—these craters and other surface markings, such as the footprints of astronauts, will remain in place for millions of years.

Astronauts took this photograph of earthrise while orbiting the moon.

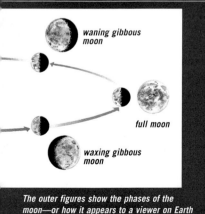

waning gibbous moon

full moon

waxing gibbous moon

The outer figures show the phases of the moon—or how it appears to a viewer on Earth in the various positions of its orbit.

Eclipses

The word "eclipse" means to hide from sight. During a solar eclipse, the sun is hidden by the moon. In a lunar eclipse the moon is hidden by Earth's shadow.

RING ECLIPSE

Sometimes a solar eclipse occurs when the moon is in the far end of its orbit. The moon's apparent size is then a little bit smaller, because it is farther away, and it doesn't completely cover the sun. A ring of sunlight appears around the edge of the sun. This is called a ring or annular eclipse.

Solar eclipse

When the new moon passes in perfect alignment between Earth and the sun, it throws two shadows: a dark inner shadow, called the umbra, that comes to a point on Earth's surface; and a lighter outer shadow, called the penumbra, that spreads over a wider area. To see a total solar eclipse you must be in the spot on Earth where the moon's inner shadow falls. If you are outside this area, but still within the outer shadow, you will see a partial eclipse.

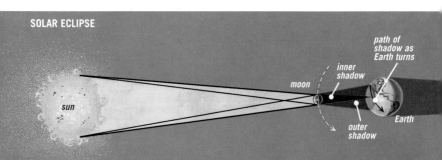

SOLAR ECLIPSE

sun

moon

inner shadow

outer shadow

path of shadow as Earth turns

Earth

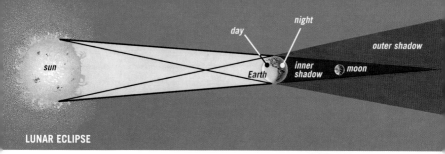

Lunar eclipse

A lunar eclipse happens when Earth's shadow falls across the full moon. During the eclipse the moon passes through Earth's outer shadow, which is faint and not always visible, and then into the inner shadow, which is heavy and darkens the moon significantly. A lunar eclipse is less dramatic than a solar eclipse, but you can look at it without risking eye damage, and it is visible to everyone on the night side of Earth.

DON'T LOOK!

A solar eclipse is a wondrous event—but don't look at it, except the moments when the sun is blocked completely. Looking directly at the sun can cause permanent damage to your eyes. Some planetariums sell special glasses made just for watching an eclipse, but regular sunglasses won't protect your eyes. You can also watch an eclipse through a pinhole viewer that you can make yourself.

To make a pinhole viewer, you need a cardboard shoe box without the top, a piece of white paper, tape, a pencil, and tinfoil. Tape the white paper on the inside of one end of the box. Cut a hole in the other end about 2 inches (5 cm) in diameter, and tape a piece of foil over the hole. Poke a hole in the foil with the pencil point. Hold the viewer up to the sun and adjust it until you see the image of the sun appear on the white paper. Make the hole larger if the image is too faint (but don't make it too big or the sun will appear blurry). When the eclipse starts, you will be able to see the moon's shadow cross in front of the sun.

Planets

Earth is the third planet out from the sun. It is one of the inner planets, along with Mercury, Venus, and Mars. The orbits of the inner planets are inside the asteroid belt, which runs between Mars and Jupiter. The planets whose orbits lie farther out are called the outer planets.

Seeing Mercury and Venus

The planets with orbits smaller than Earth's orbit—Mercury and Venus—are called inferior planets. Because they are closer to the sun than Earth, they are always fairly near the sun. That means we have to look for them near the sun but when the sky is dark—before sunrise or after sunset. They appear as bright starry objects. Venus is brighter than all the stars and all the other planets.

Venus

Mercury

PHASES OF VENUS

As Venus revolves around the sun, different parts of it appear illuminated. It goes through phases, just as our moon does. As with the moon, the phases result from the position of Venus in space with respect to the sun and Earth. When Venus is on the side of its orbit that is closer to Earth, it also appears larger and thus brighter in our sky. The crescent Venus appears large and bright because it is so close to Earth. Mercury also goes through these phases, but because it is smaller, and closer to the sun, changes in its phase and size are less apparent.

sun

Venus

Measuring elongation

crescent
moon

The distance between a planet and the sun from our viewpoint, called the planet's elongation, is measured in degrees. A full circle has 360 degrees. Mercury's elongation never gets greater than 28 degrees—that's about three of your fists held side by side (see page 44 to learn how to measure with your fist), which means you will always find Mercury within three fists of the sun. Venus, with its larger orbit, has a maximum elongation of 48 degrees—that's about five fists.

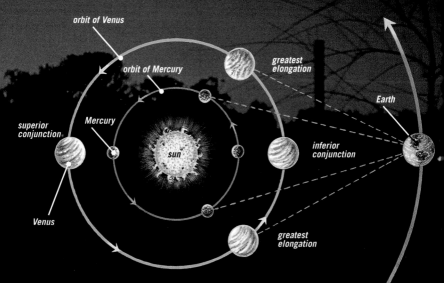

orbit of Venus

orbit of Mercury

greatest
elongation

Earth

superior
conjunction

Mercury

sun

inferior
conjunction

Venus

greatest
elongation

MERCURY AND VENUS ORBITS

As Mercury and Venus orbit the sun they pass through a series of positions from our point of view on Earth. As the illustration shows, Mercury is always very close to the sun, and its greatest elongation is very small. This means Mercury can be seen around sunrise and sunset (close to the sun), but not late at night, when the sun is gone. Venus's orbit is larger and its maximum elongation is greater, and Venus can be seen quite long before sunrise or after sunset. When one of these planets is in front of the sun or behind the sun, a position called conjunction, we cannot see it.

Superior planets

The planets whose orbits are farther away from the sun than that of Earth—Mars, Jupiter, Saturn, Uranus, Neptune, and Pluto—are called the superior planets. The superior planets travel through the zodiac but, unlike the inferior planets, are not always spotted near the sun.

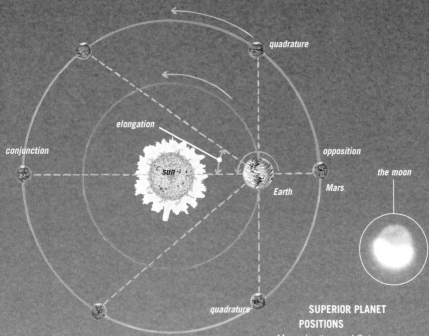

quadrature

elongation

conjunction

opposition

the moon

sun

Earth

Mars

quadrature

SUPERIOR PLANET POSITIONS

Mars, Jupiter, and Saturn are the most easily visible of the superior planets. They are farther away from the sun than Earth is, so we can see them in different parts of the sky. They can be near the sun, behind the sun (a position called conjunction), or directly opposite the sun (called opposition). We can't see them at conjunction, because the sun is in the way. They are biggest and brightest at opposition. When at opposition, they rise around sunset, are in the sky all night, and set around sunrise. When a planet's elongation is 90°, its position is called quadrature and it is visible in either the morning sky or the evening sky.

Backing up

The general direction the planets move in the sky is from west to east. But when the superior planets are near opposition, they seem to reverse direction (this is called retrograde motion) for a couple of months. This happens because the superior planets orbit more slowly than Earth, and when they are at opposition, we speed past them.

Jupiter

This drawing shows how far Earth, Mars, Jupiter, and Saturn move in their orbits in 365 days. The entire orbit is shown for each; the portion covered in 365 days is colored yellow.

Jupiter

Mars

Earth

Saturn

Saturn

Venus

This photograph shows Jupiter, Saturn, Venus, and the moon. The planets travel at different speeds in their orbits and are rarely seen so close together.

SPEEDING EARTH

The planets have different size orbits and revolve around the sun at different speeds. In the time that it takes Jupiter to make a single orbit around the sun, Earth will have completed 12 orbits. This means that the planets constantly appear in different places in the sky in relation to each other. Sometimes two, three, or even more planets will be lined up in the sky.

Mars, Saturn, and Jupiter photographed through small telescopes.

Comets, asteroids, and meteors

The sun is at the center of our solar system, and the planets orbit around it. But those aren't the only things floating around in the solar system. There are comets, asteroids, dust, and bits of rock, too. These things are all leftover debris from the solar system's origin billions of years ago.

coma

nucleus

Dirty snowballs

Comets reside in the outer solar system, in an area called the Oort Cloud. Comets are mostly ice of various compounds, especially water, mixed with rocks, rock dust, and carbon compounds. They look like huge, dirty snowballs. Occasionally one of these snowballs enters the inner solar system and comes into view of Earth.

The sun

A comet's "head" has a central nucleus surrounded by a gas cloud called the coma. As the comet approaches the sun, sunlight pushes dust particles in the coma away from the sun. This produces the dust tail, a white, gray, or sometimes yellowish tail curving away from the sun. The solar wind, charged particles that are constantly ejected from the sun, knocks electrons off some of the gas molecules in the coma and creates the ion tail, a straight bluish-white tail pointing away from the sun. Comet tails can be tens of millions of miles long.

dust tail

ion tail

Meteoroid, meteor, meteorite

Bits of dust, rock, and metal from comets and asteroids are also floating around in the solar system. These small bits and pieces are called meteoroids. They sometimes fall into Earth's atmosphere, where they usually burn up, leaving a momentary streak of light that we call a meteor or shooting star. Rarely, a very big chunk of rock and/or metal makes it all the way to the ground. This is called a meteorite.

Tiny planets

Asteroids (also called minor planets) are chunks of rock that, like the planets, orbit the sun. The largest asteroid, Ceres, is 600 miles (960 km) in diameter, but most measure less than 30 miles (50 km). Although some asteroids orbit near Earth, tens of thousands of them can be found in the asteroid belt, an orbital path located between the orbits of Mars and Jupiter.

This little asteroid, named Ida, is about 35 miles (55 km) long and has a tiny moon that revolves around it.

Celestial sphere

When you look up at the sky, it looks like a huge upside-down bowl over your head. Someone on the other side of Earth gets the same impression. If you put those two bowls together, you have a complete sphere of sky surrounding Earth. We call this the celestial (which means sky) sphere. The northern half of this sphere is called the Northern Hemisphere; the southern half is called the Southern Hemisphere.

EARTH AND SKY MOTIONS

If you watch the stars for a few hours one night, you will see that they seem to move across the sky very slowly and are in a different position at the end of your viewing period than they were when you started. But it is not the sky that you see moving; it is Earth, spinning on its central axis. The sky, reflecting Earth's rotation, seems to move in the opposite direction.

line of declination

MAPPING THE SKY

Maps of Earth have lines running from the north pole to the south pole called lines of longitude and lines going around Earth parallel to the equator called lines of latitude. Astronomers invented a similar system to help them map the sky, pinpoint the locations of stars and other objects, and aim their telescopes. In the sky, the latitude lines (running parallel to the celestial equator) are called lines of declination and the longitude lines (running pole to pole) are called lines of right ascension.

ECLIPTIC

Another great circle in the sky is the ecliptic. It represents the sun's apparent path around the celestial sphere each year. What appears to be the sun's motion is actually Earth's movement as it orbits the sun, and the ecliptic is really the plane of Earth's orbit projected onto the celestial sphere. The ecliptic runs through the constellations of the zodiac.

north celestial pole

+90°

northern celestial hemisphere

+60°

line of right ascension

+30°

0°

ecliptic

Earth

celestial equator

-30°

-60°

sun

southern celestial hemisphere

-90°

south celestial pole

POLES AND EQUATOR

You probably already know that Earth has north and south poles and an equator. The extensions of the poles and the equator out into space are called the north celestial pole, the south celestial pole, and the celestial equator.

Pretend that you are standing on Earth in the center of this drawing. Imagine that all the constellations are plastered up on the inside of the sphere. Each constellation is in a specific position on the sphere, at its own coordinates (lines of declination and right ascension). Many star maps have these coordinates mapped on them.

Finding things in the sky

Long-exposure photograph showing trails of stars that revolve around the celestial pole

If you want to tell a friend where to find your favorite star tonight, you'll have to figure out a way to give him or her directions. You may need to explain some measurements. Don't worry, there are plenty of tricks for finding objects in the sky.

Altitude is up, azimuth is around

Altitude measures how many degrees above the horizon your object is. The horizon is 0°. The zenith, the point directly over your head, is 90°. A star halfway up the sky, between the horizon and the zenith, is at an altitude of 45°. Now pretend to lay a compass on the ground. North is 0°. East is 90°. South is 180°. West is 270°. North is also 360°. These are azimuth coordinates.

Word of the day

To give directions to an object in the sky, you must know its azimuth—where along the horizon it is (north, south, east, or west)—and its altitude, or how high up in the sky it is. Combined, these are called altazimuth coordinates.

RISING STARS

Stars rise in the eastern half of the horizon, at an azimuth between 0° and 180°. When a star just peeks above the horizon, its altitude is 0°. It continues to rise at an angle, so its azimuth changes as its altitude changes. This drawing shows a star's progress over the course of a night. At each point shown, the star is at a different altitude and azimuth.

celestial meridian (line from north to south)

star rises at the horizon

North 0°/360°

star sets below the horizon

NORTH STAR

All stars, except Polaris, the North Star, change their altazimuth positions during the course of the night. Polaris is at due north, like the north pole, and that's where it stays. All the other stars in the northern sky spin around Polaris, including the other stars of its constellation, which form the Little Dipper.

GIVE YOURSELF A HAND

When you are looking up at a star, how can you tell what its altitude is? Use your hand as a measuring device. Face the sky and extend your arm straight out, with your hand up before your eyes. The average fist measures about 10° wide. Starting at the horizon, make fist measurements upward to the star. A star with an altitude of 45° is about four and a half fists high. You can use your fingers in the same way. A thumb is about 1½° and three fingers span about 5°.

Hold your pinky up in front of the full moon and line them up. The moon measures ½°, about the width of your pinky.

zenith (point directly overhead)

star's highest altitude

direction sky rotates as Earth turns

East 90°

observer measuring altitude of Polaris

South 180°

West 270°

This drawing shows, from an observer's perspective on Earth, how a star seems to rise, move up in the sky, and set over the course of a night.

Using the field guide

T his section features detailed descriptions, photographs, and sky maps of things you can see in the night sky. It begins with the solar system: the sun, the moon, planets, comets, meteors,

The moon

and man-made satellites. Next are seasonal sky maps that show the constellations of the northern sky in each of the four seasons. Maps and photographs of select constellations and the stars, nebulas, and galaxies within them follow.

ICONS
These icons, which appear on each left-hand page, help you quickly find the section you are looking for.

Solar System

Constellations

NAME
The name tells you what is covered on the page.

SUBJECT ICON
The icon identifies the subject on the page as a solar system object or a constellation.

IDENTIFICATION CAPSULE
The identification capsule gives you a description of the object and vital information about its size, brightness, and movements.

BOX HEADING
The box heading alerts you to more information on the subject covered on the main page.

VIEWING TIPS
The viewing tips explain when and where the subject can be seen and whether you can see it with the naked eye or with binoculars or a telescope.

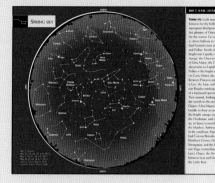

Seasonal sky map

Constellations

The constellation section of the field guide is divided into two parts: the sky in different seasons and individual constellations.

SEASONAL SKY MAPS

- The seasonal sky maps provide a full-sky view of the sky in each season, with the constellations and brightest stars labeled.
- The maps show the sky as it appears from a latitude of 40° north. If you are at a different latitude, the maps will be off by a small amount with each degree north or south of this latitude.
- Each map shows the sky at 9 p.m. at a date right in the middle of the season. To use the map on other dates, you have to go out at a different time of night. The times each map can be used appear on the lower left corner of the map.
- The zenith is marked on the season maps; this is the point directly overhead the viewer at the date and time represented by the map.
- The Milky Way appears as a wavy, light blue area on all maps.

SKY-WATCHING IN THE SOLAR SYSTEM

If you watch the sky throughout the year you will notice that the stars of a season seem to stay in place, while objects in the solar system move relatively quickly against the background of stars. The moon and planets (including Earth) move quickly and at different rates of speed. This means that they are in different parts of the sky at different times from season to season and year to year, and cannot be plotted on a sky map as the constellations and stars can be. The solar system tables in the Reference section give dates and locations of the planets over the coming years, as well as solar and lunar eclipses and meteor showers. Be sure to study part 2 of this guide (How to look at the sky) for the information on the solar system, light-years, the zodiac, magnitude, and measurements.

Orion and Canis Major

The Constellations

Following the four season maps are select individual constellations. These are constellations that have objects of interest to the amateur sky observer, such as bright stars, star clusters, galaxies, and nebulas. Like the seasonal sky maps, they are arranged by season, starting with constellations that are best viewed in spring and ending with those best viewed in winter.

Each constellation opens with a map of the constellation itself, with stars, clusters, nebulas, and galaxies labeled. Following the map are one or two spreads with photographs of the constellation and some of the interesting objects within it.

LOOKING AT CONSTELLATIONS

Before you go outside with your field guide to look at constellations, sit down with the seasonal sky map and trace the objects you want to see. Turn to the individual constellations and decide which ones you want to look at in more detail.

Once outside, find north. Hold the season map up above your head, with the north end of the map pointed toward north. Looking from the map (use a red flashlight) to the sky, find your way from one constellation to the next. It's a good idea to start in the west, because the stars in the west will set first. The circumpolar constellations, those that revolve around the north celestial pole, with Polaris in Ursa Minor at their center, never set in the Northern Hemisphere and will be up all the time, although their locations and orientations vary. Look for the zodiac, and trace the constellations that follow its arc. This is where the planets will be found.

Once you have looked at the entire sky, you may want to focus on one or two individual constellations. Find the constellation using the season map. Then turn to the map for that constellation and locate the pattern, the bright stars, and other objects marked on the maps. Turn to the next page and look at the photographs and the detailed descriptions of the constellation's highlights. For each constellation, the text gives the best viewing time, which is the period of the year when the constellation is highest in the sky in the evening, and the season maps on which you can find the constellation.

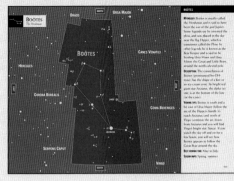

Constellation map

CONSTELLATION MAPS

- The constellation maps show the boundaries of each constellation (in orange), the bright stars and other objects (see legend, below), and the traditional connect-the-dots shape.
- On all star maps, east is on the left and west is on the right (the opposite of geographical maps). This is because when you hold the map up above your head, you have to turn it over to point it toward north, and the left and right sides get flipped. (Stand with a season map pointed to north, then raise it over your head, and turn it to point north. See how east and west end up in their usual positions?)
- Stars in constellations are labeled with Greek letters. Usually, the brightest star has the first letter of the Greek alphabet (alpha α), the next-brightest has the second letter (beta β), and so on. The stars are often referred to by these Greek letters, and some stars also have names, such as Betelgeuse (the alpha star in Orion) and Sirius (the alpha star in Canis Major).
- Many star clusters, galaxies, and nebulas are labeled with letters and/or numbers. These labels come from lists of these objects. The most famous is the Messier Catalog; all objects on this list have the letter "M" followed by a number. Other lists are the New General Catalog (NGC) and the Index Catalog (IC).

GREEK LETTERS		
α alpha	ι iota	ρ rho
β beta	κ kappa	σ sigma
γ gamma	λ lambda	τ tau
δ delta	μ mu	υ upsilon
ε epsilon	ν nu	φ phi
ζ zeta	ξ xi	χ chi
η eta	ο omicron	ψ psi
ϑ theta	π pi	ω omega

MAP LEGEND

STAR MAGNITUDES:

−1 0 1 2 3 4 5

- OPEN CLUSTERS
- GLOBULAR CLUSTERS
- BRIGHT NEBULAS
- PLANETARY NEBULAS
- GALAXIES

Although the sun is not visible in the night sky, it is a star, and the only one we can see with any detail. The daytime sky (when Earth is facing the sun) is as full of stars as the night sky, but the sun is so bright it drowns out the light of all others. Each day the sun appears to rise in the east, move across the sky, and set in the west. The sun's apparent movement is actually caused by the movement of Earth as it spins on its axis (an imaginary line running through the center of Earth), making a complete turn each 24 hours.

DESCRIPTION: The sun is a yellow-white main sequence star. It usually looks blinding white or yellowish. At sunrise or sunset it may appear orange, pink, or red; this is caused by dust, pollen, and other materials in the atmosphere, which filter out rays of blue and violet light. The sun is the brightest object in our sky, with a

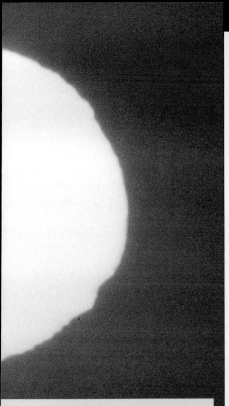

THE SUN'S DAILY PATH

DESCRIPTION: Because Earth is tilted on its axis, the northern half tilts toward the sun for half the year (spring and summer) and tilts away for the other half (fall and winter). This makes the sun's path through the sky and the place where it rises and sets appear to change over the course of a year. In spring and summer, its daily path in the sky is high and long; in fall and winter, it is low and short. **VIEWING TIPS:** Photograph or draw pictures of sunrise or sunset at different times of year with the same landmarks in the picture. You can easily see how much the sun's path moves during the year.

SUNSPOTS

DESCRIPTION: Sunspots, dark blotches on the surface of the sun, are areas that are cooler than the surrounding surface. They are caused by intense magnetic activity, which keeps energy from flowing outward. The sun has cycles of magnetic activity, going from periods of little activity to periods of high activity every 11 years. Therefore, every 11 years the sun has many sunspots. **VIEWING TIPS:** You may be able to see sunspots by projecting the sun through a pinhole viewer (see page 35).

magnitude of –27. It is 93 million miles (150 million km) from Earth.

VIEWING TIPS: Never look directly at the sun or look at it through binoculars or a telescope. You can sometimes look at it when it is filtered behind clouds or when it is low in the sky and most filtered by the atmosphere (near sunrise or sunset). If you want to watch an eclipse or find sunspots, you can make a pinhole viewer, as described on page 35.

SOLAR ECLIPSES

A solar eclipse, which occurs when the moon moves directly between Earth and the sun and briefly blocks the sun's light, is one of the most awesome celestial events. You should count yourself lucky if you get to see a total eclipse during your lifetime. Partial and ring eclipses are also thrilling to see, although not quite as dramatic.

DIAMOND RING

DESCRIPTION: Just before and after the moments when a solar eclipse is total, a bright flash of light sometimes appears, called a diamond ring. It is caused by a ray of sunlight peeking through mountains and valleys on the edge of the moon. **VIEWING TIPS:** Watch for the diamond ring through your pinhole viewer. Do not look directly at it.

RING ECLIPSE

DESCRIPTION: Another type of eclipse is a ring (or annular) eclipse. Sometimes a total solar eclipse occurs when the moon is at apogee (the part of its orbit farthest from Earth) and appears as a disk slightly smaller than the sun, enabling a ring of sunlight to shine around the dark body of the moon. **VIEWING TIPS:** Watch a ring eclipse with a pinhole viewer.

DESCRIPTION: When a total solar eclipse occurs, the sky darkens, the temperature drops, and the glorious, outermost atmosphere of the sun, the corona, becomes visible. The period when the sun's disk is completely blocked from view is called totality. If you are not in the area of the world where the total eclipse can be seen, you may be able to see a partial eclipse, in which the moon covers only part of the sun.

VIEWING TIPS: There are, on average, about two solar eclipses each year (see the table on page 152 for dates of upcoming eclipses). You can see a total solar eclipse only when the sun, moon, and Earth are in perfect alignment, and only if you are on the spot on Earth where the alignment can be seen (that is, you must be "aligned" as well). Protect your eyes when viewing a solar eclipse with special, strongly filtered glasses sold by planetariums, or by constructing a pinhole viewer (see page 35).

THE MOON
Satellite

The moon is Earth's constant companion. It is one of the few celestial bodies visible in the daytime, but the moon doesn't shine on its own. It is illuminated by the sun. Just like Earth, half of it is always in daylight and half is in darkness. As it revolves around Earth, we get different views of its day side; these are the phases of the moon.

DESCRIPTION: The moon is a planetlike satellite that revolves around Earth, completing one orbit every 29½ days. When the moon is between Earth and the sun, it is very near the sun and invisible to us; this is called a new moon. A crescent moon is a thin sliver of moon; a half (or quarter) moon is a half circle; a gibbous moon is more than half lit.

VIEWING TIPS: When the moon is full, it rises when the sun sets and sets when the sun rises. It is in the sky all night. Sometimes a rising full moon looks huge as it peeks above the horizon, through trees or over buildings. If you measure it with your finger (see page 44) at moonrise, and later when it looks high and small in the sky, you will see that it is exactly the same size. It only looks big when compared with the trees and houses as it rises. At new moon, when the moon is in the sky all day and very near the sun (from our viewpoint), it is invisible. The moon rises almost an hour later each day in its cycle: Between new moon and full moon, it rises in the day and sets at night; after full moon, it rises at night and sets in the day.

HALF MOON

DESCRIPTION: A half moon is also called a quarter moon because we see one half of the lit half, which is one quarter. **VIEWING TIPS:** The half moon happens twice a month, a week before and a week after full moon. The first-quarter moon (before full moon) rises at noon and sets at midnight, while the third-quarter moon (after full moon) rises at midnight and sets at noon.

CRESCENT MOON

DESCRIPTION: When the moon is a crescent, the unlit part of the moon is often visible. This is called earthshine, and is due to light reflecting off Earth's atmosphere. It is also called "the old moon in the new moon's arms." **VIEWING TIPS:** Earthshine is visible just before and after new moon.

NORTH

LUNAR LANDSCAPE

W. Bond

MARE FRIGORIS

Harpalus   Bianchini   Plato   ALPES   Aristoteles

SINUS
RORIS

SINUS
IRIDUM

Pico   Eudoxus

Vallis Alpes   MONTES

Mairan   Cassini

MARE IMBRIUM

Aristillus

Archimedes   Autolycus

Otto Struve   MARE S

Lambert

*Vallis
Schröteri*   Aristarchus   Euler   Timocharis   MARE S

Herodotus   Wallace   MONTES APENNINUS

Seleucus   Mene

MONTES CARPATUS   Eratosthenis   Manilius

Marius   SINUS
AESTUUM   MARE
VAPORUM

Kepler   Copernicus   Julius

SINUS
MEDII   Agrip

OCEANUS
PROCELLARUM   Reinhold   Triesnecker   Godin

Riccioli   Lansberg   Delamt

Fra Mauro   Herschel   Hipparchus

Grimaldi   MONTES
RIPHAEUS   Ptolemaeus

Crüger   Albategnius

MARE COGNITUM   Alphonsus   Abulfeda

Gassendi   Alpetragius   Tac

Bulliadus   Arzachel   Ca

Mersenius   MARE
NUBIUM   Playfair-G

MARE
HUMORUM   Purbach   Sac

Regiomontanus   Apianus

Vieta   Campanus   Pitatus   Aliacensis

Mercator   Walter   Werner

Cichus   Fabricius

Capuanus   Gauricus

Wurzelbauer

Schickard   Maurolycus

Wilhelm   Stöfler

Tycho   Faraday

Schiller   Cuvier   Pitis

Phocylides   Longomontanus   Homm

Scheiner   Clavius

Blancanus

SOUTH

Endymion

Hercules Atlas

Cepheus Messala

Franklin

Geminus

nius Burckhardt

ATIS Cleomedes

Vitruvius Macrobius **MARE CRISIUM**

Plinius Proclus

Condorcet

RE TRANQUILLITATIS

Firmicus

Tarantius

er Maskelyne Appolonius

Sabine

MARE FECUNDITATIS

Langrenus

Capella Gutenberg

hilus Mädler Goclenius

us

MARE NECTARIS Colombo

Santbech Vendelinus

RUPES ALTAI Fracastorius

Petavius

Snellius

Piccolomini Stevinus Furnerius

Rheita

i Levi Metius *Vallis Rheita*

Fabricius

Jansen

Vlacq

DESCRIPTION: When you look up at the moon you may see dark and light blotches that make the shape of a face—the "man in the moon." Those marks are actually valleys, mountains, craters, and other features, similar to the geological features on Earth. Each huge dark area is a "mare" (plural "maria"), which means sea. These seas are not of water, but of hardened lava. Around some of the craters, which look like small rings, you can see bright splashes of material that was splattered when meteorites crashed into the moon. This map shows some of the landscape features on the moon's surface that can be seen from Earth.

VIEWING TIPS: The best time to look at the moon's landforms is when the moon is not full. At full moon it can be too bright for much detail to show. Look at a half, crescent, or gibbous moon near the terminator, which is the area between the moon's sunlit part and the part that is not lit (and that you can't see). If you look with binoculars, some of the moon's features will look "3-D" (three-dimensional). With a telescope you can see many of the craters and mountains.

LUNAR ECLIPSES

L unar eclipses occur when Earth lines up exactly between the sun and the full moon, and the moon moves through Earth's shadow.

DESCRIPTION: When a lunar eclipse starts, you can see Earth's shadow slowly creeping across the moon. Earth's shadow is about three times larger than the moon, and it can take more than three hours for the moon to cross the shadow.

VIEWING TIPS: Lunar eclipses happen about twice a year during a full moon. They are visible from all over the night side of Earth, not just a small area as with solar eclipses, and you need no equipment to see them. See the table on page 152 for dates of upcoming eclipses. They are usually announced in newspapers and on news shows, as well as in astronomy magazines.

ECLIPSE COLORS

DESCRIPTION: Even when the moon is completely covered by Earth's shadow (totality) it often does not go completely black. Sometimes it has a reddish glow throughout totality. This color comes from light rays in Earth's atmosphere. **VIEWING TIPS:** The moon's color during totality depends on the cloud cover on Earth.

PARTIAL LUNAR ECLIPSE

DESCRIPTION: A partial lunar eclipse occurs when only part of Earth's shadow passes across the full moon. **VIEWING TIPS:** A partial lunar eclipse lasts an hour or two. Watch for the shape of Earth's shadow on the moon. Because Earth is a sphere, it produces a curved, dark shadow. It is from the shadow that the ancient Greeks figured out that Earth was a globe.

59

Mercury

ercury is the closest planet to the sun, the second smallest planet (if we count Pluto), and by far the speediest. Noting that it completes its orbit around the sun in only 88 days, ancient stargazers named it after the fleet-footed messenger god.

DESCRIPTION: Mercury can be hard to spot because it orbits so near the sun, and the sun often hides it from view. But when Mercury is at its greatest elongation (the farthest it gets from the sun from our viewpoint), it can be one of the brightest objects in the sky. In this photograph, Mercury is the pale object right in the center; Venus, Jupiter, and the moon are at the top right.

DISTANCE FROM SUN: 36 million miles (58 million km). **DIAMETER:** 3,031 miles (4,878 km). **MAGNITUDE:** +1 to –1.5. **SATELLITES:** None.

TELESCOPE VIEW

DESCRIPTION: Mercury is so small and far from Earth, and so often lost in the sun's glare, that we can't see any details, even with a telescope. This picture of Mercury, shown partially illuminated by the sun in a quarter phase, was taken through a telescope. **VIEWING TIPS:** If you look at Mercury through binoculars you may be able to see its silvery color. Mercury's phases, which change as it orbits the sun, can be observed with a telescope.

SURFACE AND ATMOSPHERE

DESCRIPTION: Mercury has essentially no atmosphere and its surface temperature ranges from a blistering 700°F (400°C) to an icy cold –274°F (–170°C). The above photograph of Mercury's pockmarked landscape was transmitted to Earth by the *Mariner 10* mission. **VIEWING TIPS:** Mercury's surface is not clear from Earth, even through binoculars or a telescope.

VIEWING TIPS: Mercury appears as a bright starlike object in the early morning just before the rising sun or in evening twilight just after the sun sets. Check the table on page 153 for dates of Mercury's appearances. Search the horizon about 16°–27° (about 1½ to 3 fists) above and left of the setting sun (above and right if it is rising). If you don't find it, try again at its next appearance.

Venus is the brightest object in the sky after the sun and the moon, with a magnitude of about −4. In this photograph, taken at dusk, Venus appears at top left— even in twilight, its brilliance shines through.

DESCRIPTION: The closest planet to Earth, Venus looks like a very bright star to the naked eye. Like Mercury, when Venus is at its greatest elongation it appears at either dusk or dawn. But Venus is farther from the sun than Mercury, and so can be seen relatively late at night or long before sunrise. Venus is sometimes called the Morning Star or the Evening Star, depending on what time of day it appears.

DISTANCE FROM SUN: 67 million miles (108 million km). **DIAMETER:** 7,520 miles (12,100 km). **MAGNITUDE:** −4 to −4.5. **SATELLITES:** None.

VIEWING TIPS: Check the chart on page 153 for dates and times that Venus is visible. It is always 48° or less from the sun, or about 5 fists from the horizon at sunrise or sunset. You can sometimes see Venus in broad daylight: When it is visible at dawn, measure off its distance from the sun, using your fist as a measuring instrument. Later in the day, look for it by marking off the measurement you made earlier. The phases of Venus are visible with good binoculars or a telescope. Venus is half full at its greatest elongations.

SURFACE

DESCRIPTION: The surface of Venus is covered with mountains, valleys, volcanoes, lava, and craters. In this image of the planet, created from data gathered by the *Magellan* spacecraft, bright areas are rugged terrain, including mountains and lava flows, and dark areas are smooth and include plains. **VIEWING TIPS:** Venus's surface cannot be seen from Earth, even through a telescope.

ATMOSPHERE

DESCRIPTION: Venus is covered in a thick, cloudy atmosphere composed mostly of carbon dioxide. It traps heat from the sun, giving Venus the hottest surface of all the planets, with an average temperature of 900°F (500°C). **VIEWING TIPS:** Venus's atmosphere (shown here in a *Mariner 10* photograph) reflects light and is part of the reason why Venus is so bright.

Named for the Roman god of war, Mars is the planet that has most captured human interest and imagination. At times it gets brighter and takes on an orange-red hue. This change troubled early observers of the sky, who thought it meant the gods were angry with humans. Worry turned to outright fear as Mars reversed its direction (called "retrograde motion") just when its brightness and color reached their frightful peaks. Sometimes Mars' red color can't be seen at all, as in this photograph. Here Mars brightly outshines the stars of Taurus with a steady light. That steadiness—instead of twinkling—is one way to know you have spotted a planet rather than a star.

DESCRIPTION: The "red planet" varies in color intensity and brightness as it makes its way around the sun. When it is farthest from Earth it looks whitish and has a magnitude of 2. When it is closer to Earth it rivals Jupiter's brightness, and at magnitude –2, its color is obvious. At this time it also appears, over several months, to reverse the direction it is moving in the sky. This is because Earth moves faster in orbit than Mars, and when it

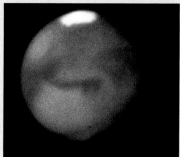

POLAR ICE CAPS

DESCRIPTION: In this telescope photograph of Mars, you can see through the planet's thin atmosphere to the surface in places. The white region at the top is a polar ice cap of frozen water and carbon dioxide.
VIEWING TIPS: Mars's two polar ice caps are visible through Earth-based telescopes. The ice caps grow during the Martian winter, shrinking back in spring.

SURFACE

DESCRIPTION: The red planet gets its color from iron oxides (rust) that blanket its surface and turn its sky pink. This photograph of Mars's rocky terrain was taken by the *Pathfinder* spacecraft. Mars's surface has volcanic formations and channels where water once flowed. **VIEWING TIPS:** When Mars is at its biggest and brightest, its color can be seen with the naked eye.

passes close by, Mars appears to move backwards.

DISTANCE FROM SUN: 142 million miles (228 million km). **DIAMETER:** 4,217 miles (6,786 km). **MAGNITUDE:** +2 to −2. **SATELLITES:** 2, Phobos (fear) and Deimos (panic), named after the dogs of the god Mars.

VIEWING TIPS: About once every two years, Mars appears opposite the sun at sunset and its reddish glow is the brightest light in the night sky. As with all the planets, it travels through the constellations of the zodiac. Look at the chart on page 153 to see where and when Mars will appear in the sky.

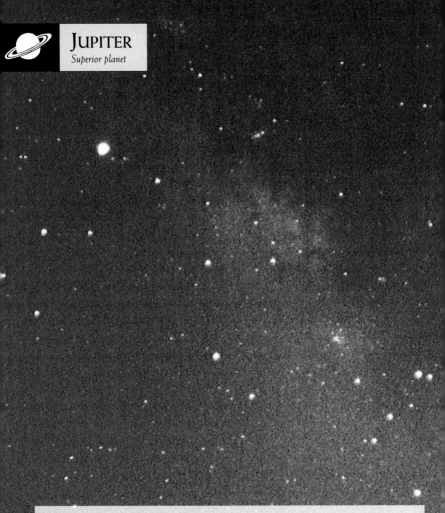

The largest of the planets, Jupiter is more than 11 times the size of Earth. It is the second brightest planet (after Venus), holding fairly steady at around –2.5 magnitude. This brightness is sometimes rivaled by Mars, but only when Earth and Mars are close in their orbits. Jupiter's brightness doesn't vary as much because it is so far away. Jupiter is the brightest object in this photograph, which also shows the Milky Way.

DESCRIPTION: It takes Jupiter 12 years to complete an orbit around the sun, but just 10 hours to complete a rotation on its axis. The rapid night-to-night movement of Venus and Mercury, with their smaller, faster orbits, offers a ready way to identify them as planets, because their movement against the backdrop of stars can be detected in a single night. Jupiter's orbit is so large and it moves so slowly that its motion among the stars is not readily evident.

DISTANCE FROM SUN: 483.7 million miles (778.3 million km). **DIAMETER:** 88,735 miles (142,800 km). **MAGNITUDE:** −2 to −3. **SATELLITES:** 16.

VIEWING TIPS: See page 153 to find out where to locate Jupiter in the zodiac. Jupiter is visible for five months at a time, with a three-month interval between appearances when it slips from view behind the sun. The only star close to Jupiter in brightness is bluish-white Sirius, the brightest star in the night sky, at −1.4 magnitude. Jupiter is white and does not twinkle like stars do.

ATMOSPHERE

DESCRIPTION: Jupiter's atmosphere is mostly hydrogen and helium, with small amounts of ammonia, methane, water vapor, and hydrocarbons. The swift spin of Jupiter on its axis swirls these colorful gases into bands around the planet, as shown in this Hubble Space Telescope image. Jupiter has a rocky metallic core surrounded by a mantle of liquid metallic hydrogen. **VIEWING TIPS:** Jupiter is the fastest spinning planet. A patient observer with a telescope may see the atmosphere change over several hours.

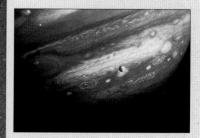

GREAT RED SPOT

DESCRIPTION: A storm has been raging on Jupiter at least since the 1600s! The red spot in the atmosphere seen behind the moon Io (on the left side of this picture, taken by *Voyager 1*) is a storm that is twice as big as Earth. The storm sometimes weakens but always comes on strong again. The moon Europa is to the right. **VIEWING TIPS:** The Great Red Spot can be seen with a medium-size telescope.

JUPITER'S MOONS
Planetary satellites

F our of the largest satellites in the solar system belong to the largest planet. These four were the first satellites to be discovered with a telescope (by Galileo in 1609). Their names, in order outward from Jupiter, are Io, Europa, Ganymede, and Callisto.

DESCRIPTION: When Jupiter is visible you can often see some of the four largest moons, depending on where each is in its orbit. Jupiter's 12 other moons are too faint to be seen with amateur instruments.

VIEWING TIPS: Some very sharp-eyed people claim to be able to see some of Jupiter's moons with the naked eye, but most of us need help. With binoculars you can see up to four of the moons. Look at the chart on page 153 for where Jupiter currently appears in the zodiac. As each moon orbits around Jupiter at a different rate of speed, the number of moons visible at any one time varies according to their positions. If you view them over a few hours you may see them move along in their orbits.

Io

DESCRIPTION: Jupiter's innermost satellite, Io, is just slightly bigger than our moon, and revolves around its giant planet once every 1¾ days. Io is covered with dark splotches of charred material spewed out by volcanoes (as shown in this *Galileo* spacecraft photograph), and has more volcanic activity than any other planet or moon in our solar system. **VIEWING TIPS:** Of the four large satellites, Io is the closest to Jupiter and the most difficult to see.

EUROPA

DESCRIPTION: Europa is the smallest of the four large moons, but is only a little smaller than our moon. It orbits Jupiter in 3½ days. *Galileo* spacecraft images of Europa, such as this one, show that this moon has a cracked icy surface that in places is floating over below-surface oceans. The presence of oceans raises the possibility that Europa might support life. **VIEWING TIPS:** Of the large satellites, Europa is second closest to Jupiter.

SATURN
Superior planet

Fainter than Venus, Jupiter, Sirius, and Mars (at maximum), Saturn is still brighter than most of the brightest stars in the sky. Because its orbit is so much larger than Earth's, its magnitude of about 0.5 remains fairly constant. Find it with binoculars and you will notice a faint yellow cast to its light. You may also be able to pick up something else—Titan, its largest satellite and the second largest of the solar system, after Jupiter's moon Ganymede.

DESCRIPTION: Saturn is the second largest planet and nearly 10 times the size of Earth. Its small rocky metallic core is surrounded by an atmosphere of liquid hydrogen.

DISTANCE FROM SUN: 885 million miles (1.427 billion km). **DIAMETER:** 74,980 (120,660 km). **MAGNITUDE:** 0 to 1.

Saturn's moons

DESCRIPTION: This dramatic mosaic of images transmitted from *Voyager* shows six of Saturn's moons. Dione (foreground) appears greatly enlarged, but Titan (upper right) is actually the largest, and is bigger even than Mercury. **VIEWING TIPS:** Titan can sometimes be seen with binoculars. The moon Rhea can be seen with a small telescope. Other moons require larger instruments.

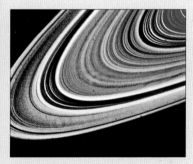

Saturn's rings

DESCRIPTION: Saturn is encircled by rings made of dust, rocks, and ice ranging in size from tiny particles to 6 feet (2 meters) across. The rings stretch 260,000 miles (416,000 km) into space, but are thought to be less than 100 yards (93 meters) thick. **VIEWING TIPS:** You need a telescope to see Saturn's rings, but even the smallest will do the job.

SATELLITES: 22.

VIEWING TIPS: See page 153 to find out when and where to spot Saturn in the sky. Its orbit around the sun takes so long (30 Earth years!) that you can observe it in the same constellation for about two years. With a small telescope you can see Saturn's fabulous ring system, an awesome sight to behold.

URANUS, NEPTUNE, AND PLUTO

Superior planets

The outermost planets— Uranus, Neptune, and Pluto—were all discovered by people using telescopes.

DESCRIPTION: Uranus is barely visible to the naked eye. Its magnitude is just brighter than 6, and its color is bluish. Neptune, also bluish, is fainter (magnitude 8), and best viewed with a telescope. Pluto (magnitude 14) can be seen only with a powerful telescope. More than 3 billion miles away and only two-thirds the size of our moon, Pluto is the smallest and farthest planet. Many astronomers now consider it a lump of rocky, icy material rather than a planet.

VIEWING TIPS: You need sharp eyes and an absence of light pollution

Uranus

to see Uranus. It can be found in the constellations Capricornus and Aquarius until 2009. Use binoculars, and look for the planet's bluish tint. To find Neptune, you need a small telescope. It is in Capricornus until 2009. Pluto can be seen only with a high-power telescope.

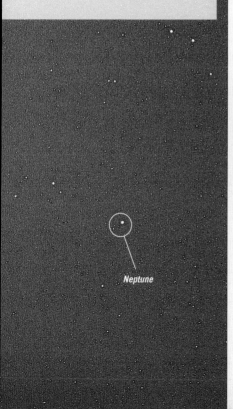

Neptune

URANUS

DESCRIPTION: One of the gas giants, Uranus is the third largest planet, four times the size of Earth. Its atmosphere contains methane, which absorbs orange-red light and reflects blue light back to Earth. **DISTANCE FROM SUN:** 1.784 billion miles (2.871 billion km). **DIAMETER:** 31,765 miles (51,118 km). **MAGNITUDE:** 5.5 to 6. **SATELLITES:** 17.

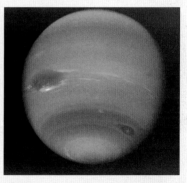

NEPTUNE

DESCRIPTION: Neptune is also a gas giant. It has a huge storm in its atmosphere (the dark blue area on the left in this *Voyager* 2 image). This storm is called the Great Dark Spot and has winds up to 1,200 mph (2,000 kph)! **DISTANCE FROM SUN:** 2.794 billion miles (4.497 billion km). **DIAMETER:** 30,750 miles (49,500 km). **MAGNITUDE:** 7.5 to 8. **SATELLITES:** 8.

73

COMETS

Comets are visible to the naked eye almost every year, and a bright one passes by once or twice a decade. Comet Hale-Bopp (pictured) made a spectacular appearance in 1996–97 and was visible to the naked eye for more than 17 months. Comets have enormous orbits, and it takes some of them thousands of years to come back our way again. Comet Hale-Bopp last appeared more than 4,000 years ago and won't return until the year 4300!

DESCRIPTION: Composed of frozen gases and rock, comets are leftover pieces from the formation of our solar system billions of years ago. Comets appear in our skies as they near the sun in their orbit and fade from our view as they continue on their journeys. Nearing the sun, their surfaces heat up and jet out huge plumes

of gas and dust, creating the brilliant tails that can stretch 60 million miles (96.5 million km).

VIEWING TIPS: Check an astronomy magazine or Web site for information on upcoming visible comets. Comets do not streak across the sky but appear still. Over several nights you should be able to detect a comet's movement against the starry background.

COMET TAILS

DESCRIPTION: This image shows Comet West (which appeared in 1976) with its two tails—one yellowish and one bluish. The yellow tail is composed of dust blown off of the comet as it nears the sun in its orbit. The blue ion tail is gas blown back from the comet by solar winds. **VIEWING TIPS:** If you have a chance to see a comet, try to see the two tails. The dust tail appears white or yellowish and may curve; the ion tail appears bluish and straight.

COMET HALLEY

DESCRIPTION: In 1682, Edmond Halley studied a comet he believed had appeared before. His work—and the comet—became famous when the comet returned when he had predicted, 76 years later. Halley used Isaac Newton's theories of gravity and motion to make his prediction. Comet Halley last appeared in 1986, and won't be back until 2061. You may be around to see it! **VIEWING TIPS:** Many comets, like Halley's, are periodical, which means they return in a specific time period.

An aurora is an amazing nighttime lighting effect that fills the sky with beautiful colors. These shimmering sky lights occur most often near Earth's north and south magnetic poles. Auroras centered on the north pole are called the aurora borealis, or northern lights, and those around the south pole are called the aurora australis, or southern lights.

AURORA SHAPES

DESCRIPTION: This picture of the aurora borealis was taken near the magnetic north pole. The shimmering cloudlike streams of light show where solar wind particles are streaming into Earth's upper atmosphere. Auroras are named for the Roman goddess of the dawn. **VIEWING TIPS:** Auroras can look like curtains of light, arcs of color, or glowing rays.

SOLAR ACTIVITY

DESCRIPTION: Auroras occur at all times near the magnetic poles. Away from the poles they increase in frequency during periods of numerous sunspots and flares and other solar activity. **VIEWING TIPS:** Periods of high solar activity, and more auroras, tend to occur every 11 years. The years 2000 and 2011, and every 11 years thereafter, are likely to see peaks of solar activity.

DESCRIPTION: Auroras occur when electrically charged particles from the sun, called solar wind, interact with Earth's magnetic field. Such particles flow from the sun all the time. Solar flares send out extra-energetic blasts of these particles. When the solar wind reaches Earth, the particles crash into particles of our upper atmosphere, energizing them. When the particles de-energize, they lose their energy in the form of light. That's what you see as the aurora. The different colors represent different amounts of energy released by different elements.

VIEWING TIPS: Auroras can be seen most frequently near the north and south poles. They are sometimes visible as far south as the southern United States. Look for reports of extra-high solar activity.

Meteoroids are fragments of rock and metal that fly through space. Called meteors when they enter Earth's upper atmosphere, they burn up as they descend, leaving a streak of light across the sky, often called a shooting or falling star. A piece large enough to strike Earth's surface is known as a meteorite.

DESCRIPTION: Meteoroids usually range in size from tiny particles, the size of a grain of sand, to marble-sized bits. A meteor shower occurs when Earth passes through a trail of material left across its orbital path by a comet. There may be tons of particles. Most disintegrate harmlessly from the tremendous friction and heat built up as they fall through the atmosphere. Very large meteors that soar through the sky in a big flash (such as the one pictured) are called fireballs.

VIEWING TIPS: On any moonless night you should be able to spot several meteors. Binoculars won't help—meteors are too quick. The table on page 152 lists dates of major meteor showers. Meteors fall more heavily after midnight than before.

METEOR SHOWERS

DESCRIPTION: Meteor showers occur at the same time each year when Earth passes a debris-filled spot in its orbit. The showers are named for the constellation they appear to come from. This photograph shows the Perseid meteor shower (August 10–13), from the constellation Perseus.

VIEWING TIPS: If a meteor shower is predicted, find the constellation on the seasonal sky map and go watch the show!

METEORITES

DESCRIPTION: Meteorites, materials from space that strike Earth's surface, are rare and usually fall harmlessly and unnoticed. However, large meteorites have struck Earth with amazing force. About 50,000 years ago, one landed in Arizona that left a crater ¾ mile (1.2 km) wide and 570 feet (170 meters) deep. The meteorite pictured, from the Arizona crater, is composed of iron. **VIEWING TIPS:** Many museums have meteorites on display.

79

MAN-MADE SATELLITES

Thousands of man-made satellites have been sent into space since the first one, the Soviet Union's *Sputnik*, was launched in 1957. Satellites do many things, including monitor weather, study space, send TV signals to satellite dishes, search for natural resources, and track military movements. Most of them are unnoticeable to the naked eye. The first satellite that was easily visible from Earth was a large mylar radio reflector called *Echo 1*, launched in 1960.

DESCRIPTION: On almost any clear evening you can see at least one satellite drifting across the sky, even if you live in an urban area. Typically, satellites look like stars of magnitude 2 to 4, changing brightness as they tumble. Among the brightest satellites are the Russian space station *Mir*, the U.S. space shuttle, and the International Space Station. These can be brighter than stars. A new network of 66 communication satellites called the Iridium System occasionally flares for several seconds. These flares can be brighter than Venus (–4 magnitude).

VIEWING TIPS: The best times for ground observers to see satellites are the hour of darkness after sunset and the hour of darkness before sunrise. At these times the ground is dark, but the orbiting satellites are so high up they catch the rays of the sun. Newspapers and Web sites run announcements about space shuttle launchings and visibility of other satellites.

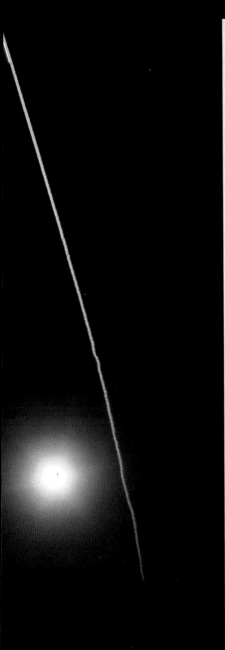

SATELLITE TRAILS

DESCRIPTION: The delicate trails of satellites can drift across any part of the sky. Two streaks appear in the above photograph. Most satellites orbit Earth 200 to 300 miles (320–480 km) up, and travel at 18,000 miles per hour (30,000 kph), completing an orbit in 1½ hours. **VIEWING TIPS:** Satellites are about as bright as stars and their light is white. (Airplanes often have colored lights.) Most satellites move in a straight, steady line across the sky.

SPACE SHUTTLE TRAIL

DESCRIPTION: The U.S. space shuttle streaks across the sky in a bright flash of light. The large photograph at left shows the shuttle *Columbia* and the moon. After the shuttle passes you can sometimes see a trail of atoms glowing in the atmosphere (pictured above). **VIEWING TIPS:** Space shuttle launchings (and reentries) are usually announced in newspapers and on news shows.

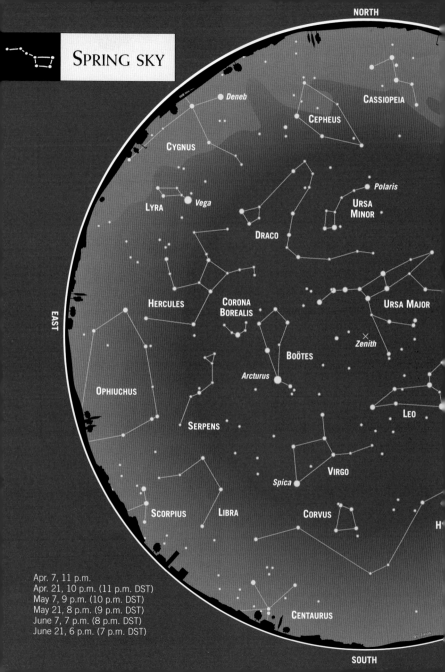

NORTH

SPRING SKY

Deneb

CASSIOPEIA

CEPHEUS

CYGNUS

Polaris

Vega

URSA MINOR

LYRA

DRACO

URSA MAJOR

EAST

HERCULES

CORONA BOREALIS

Zenith

BOÖTES

Arcturus

LEO

OPHIUCHUS

SERPENS

VIRGO

Spica

SCORPIUS

LIBRA

CORVUS

H

Apr. 7, 11 p.m.
Apr. 21, 10 p.m. (11 p.m. DST)
May 7, 9 p.m. (10 p.m. DST)
May 21, 8 p.m. (9 p.m. DST)
June 7, 7 p.m. (8 p.m. DST)
June 21, 6 p.m. (7 p.m. DST)

CENTAURUS

SOUTH

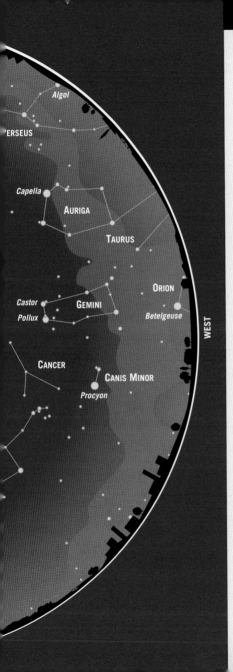

VIEWING TIPS: Look near the western horizon for the brilliant red supergiant Betelgeuse. This is the last glimpse of Orion, the Hunter, for the season. Go straight above it, about halfway to the zenith, to find Gemini's twin stars, Castor and Pollux. North of Castor is the bright star Capella (constellation Auriga, the Charioteer). The head of Ursa Major, the Great Bear, also points to Capella. South of Pollux is the bright star Procyon (in Canis Minor, the Little Dog). Between Procyon and the zenith is Leo, the Lion, with the bright star Regulus marking the bottom of a backward question mark. Turn around, looking up and over the zenith to the north to the Big Dipper (Ursa Major). Use its handle to draw an arc to Arcturus, the bright orange star of Boötes, the Herdsman, and continue the arc to Spica (constellation Virgo, the Maiden), halfway up the sky in the southeast. East of Boötes find Corona Borealis, the Northern Crown; Hercules, the Strongman; and the bluish-white star Vega (constellation Lyra, the Lyre). Draco, the Dragon, lies between Lyra and Ursa Minor, the Little Bear.

83

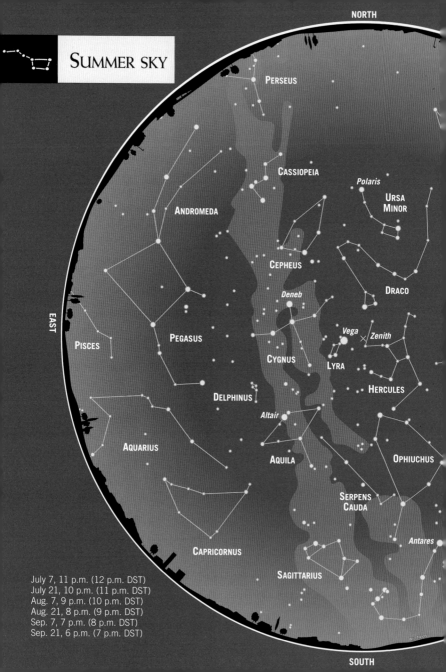

NORTH

SUMMER SKY

PERSEUS

CASSIOPEIA

Polaris

URSA
MINOR

ANDROMEDA

CEPHEUS

DRACO

Deneb

PEGASUS

Vega   ✕ *Zenith*

PISCES

LYRA

CYGNUS

HERCULES

DELPHINUS

Altair

AQUARIUS

AQUILA

OPHIUCHUS

SERPENS
CAUDA

CAPRICORNUS

Antares

SAGITTARIUS

EAST

July 7, 11 p.m. (12 p.m. DST)
July 21, 10 p.m. (11 p.m. DST)
Aug. 7, 9 p.m. (10 p.m. DST)
Aug. 21, 8 p.m. (9 p.m. DST)
Sep. 7, 7 p.m. (8 p.m. DST)
Sep. 21, 6 p.m. (7 p.m. DST)

SOUTH

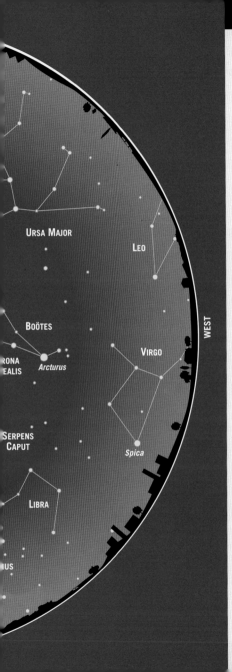

URSA MAJOR

LEO

BOÖTES

VIRGO

RONA
EALIS

Arcturus

SERPENS
CAPUT

Spica

LIBRA

US

WEST

VIEWING TIPS: Start with the pattern of the Big Dipper (constellation Ursa Major, the Great Bear) in the northwest. Trace a curve southwest from its handle to find the star Arcturus, of Boötes, the Herdsman, and then on to Spica, the bright star of Virgo, the Maiden, low in the west. Turn south to see the red supergiant star Antares in Scorpius. East of the Scorpion's tail lies the teapot shape of Sagittarius, the Archer. Scan the Milky Way, which runs behind Scorpius and Sagittarius and upward to Aquila (the Eagle), Cygnus (the Swan), Cepheus (the King), and on to Cassiopeia (the Queen) in the northeast. Straight up at the zenith lies the brilliant star Vega (in Lyra, the Lyre), the brightest corner of the Summer Triangle. Deneb (in Cygnus) and Altair (in Aquila) mark the other corners. West of Vega, directly overhead, is Hercules, the Strongman. Delphinus, the Dolphin, is northeast of Altair. East of Cassiopeia lies V-shaped Andromeda, the Princess, home of the Andromeda Galaxy. Pegasus, the Winged Horse, joins Andromeda at one corner of its Great Square.

85

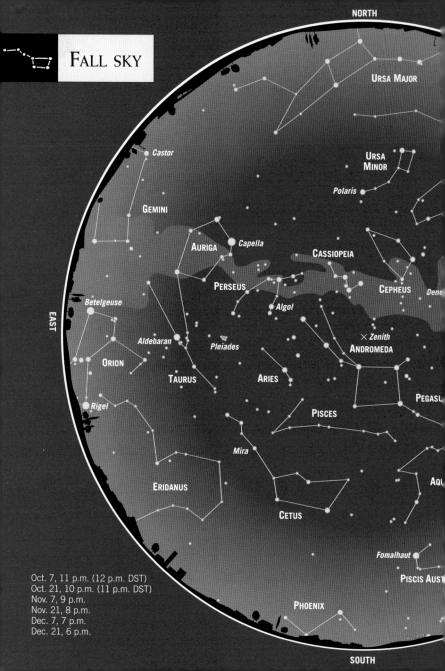

NORTH

FALL SKY

URSA MAJOR

URSA
MINOR

Polaris

Castor

GEMINI

AURIGA   Capella   CASSIOPEIA

PERSEUS   CEPHEUS   Dene

Betelgeuse   Algol

EAST   × Zenith
                                              ANDROMEDA
          Aldebaran   Pleiades

ORION   ARIES   PEGASU

TAURUS

Rigel   PISCES

                                                              AQU
          Mira

ERIDANUS

                    CETUS

                                        Fomalhaut

Oct. 7, 11 p.m. (12 p.m. DST)   PISCIS AUST
Oct. 21, 10 p.m. (11 p.m. DST)
Nov. 7, 9 p.m.
Nov. 21, 8 p.m.   PHOENIX
Dec. 7, 7 p.m.
Dec. 21, 6 p.m.

SOUTH

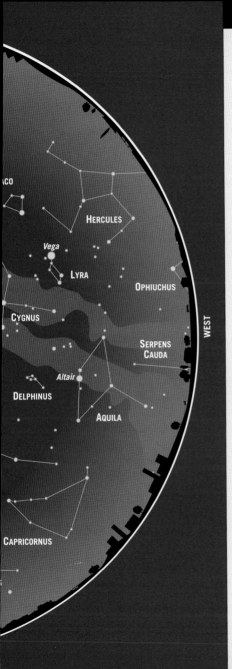

NOVEMBER 7, 9 P.M.

VIEWING TIPS: The Summer Triangle is now in the west: the brilliant star Vega in the small but distinctive constellation Lyra, the Lyre; bright star Deneb, in the constellation Cygnus, the Swan, above it; and the star Altair, in constellation Aquila, the Eagle, to the south. The little Dolphin, Delphinus, appears to leap in the sky above Altair. Locate the Milky Way, running from Aquila, up through Cygnus, past the zenith, and eastward to Auriga, the Charioteer, where it begins to weaken. Find Auriga's bright star, Capella. Taurus, the Bull, beside Auriga, and the pretty rising stars of Orion, the Hunter, due east, herald the coming of the richest celestial season, winter. Find the most famous star cluster in the sky, the Pleiades (or Seven Sisters), in Taurus. Gathered near the zenith are Cepheus, the King; Cassiopeia, the Queen; Andromeda, the Princess; Perseus, the Hero; and Pegasus, the Winged Horse, all characters in a mythological tale. Look for the Andromeda Galaxy, in Andromeda, and the star Algol, in Perseus.

87

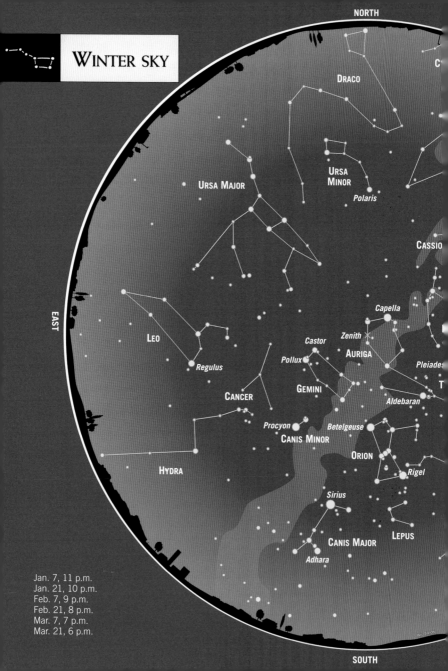

NORTH

WINTER SKY

DRACO

URSA MINOR

Polaris

URSA MAJOR

CASSIO

C

Capella

Zenith

AURIGA

Castor

LEO

Pleiades

Pollux

T

Regulus

GEMINI

Aldebaran

CANCER

Betelgeuse

Procyon

CANIS MINOR

ORION

Rigel

HYDRA

Sirius

LEPUS

CANIS MAJOR

Adhara

EAST

Jan. 7, 11 p.m.
Jan. 21, 10 p.m.
Feb. 7, 9 p.m.
Feb. 21, 8 p.m.
Mar. 7, 7 p.m.
Mar. 21, 6 p.m.

SOUTH

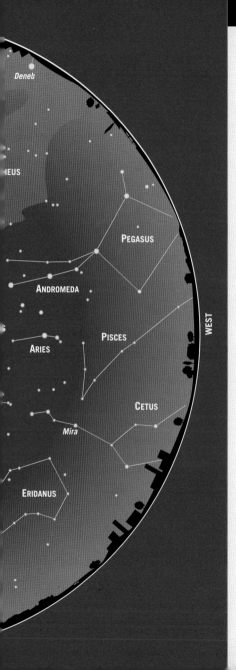

VIEWING TIPS: The bright pattern of Orion, the Hunter, halfway up in the south, features the red star Betelgeuse and the blue star Rigel. Look for the Orion Nebula in the sword, which hangs from Orion's belt. Use Orion's three belt stars to draw a line southeast to the brightest of all stars, Sirius, in the constellation Canis Major, the Great Dog. Follow the belt stars northwest to the red giant star Aldebaran, in Taurus, the Bull. Taurus has two star clusters, the Pleiades and the Hyades. East of Betelgeuse lies the brilliant star, Procyon, in Canis Minor, the Little Dog. Northeast of Procyon is the faint constellation Cancer, the Crab. Near the zenith is the bright star Capella, in Auriga, the Charioteer. The Big Dipper, part of Ursa Major, the Great Bear, lies in the northeast. The pointer stars on its cup lead to the North Star, Polaris (in Ursa Minor, the Little Bear or the Little Dipper). In the other direction the pointers lead to Leo, the Lion, and its bright star Regulus. In the northwest lies Cassiopeia, the Queen, and above it Perseus, the Hero, with its "blinking" star, Algol. To the west is Andromeda, the Princess.

89

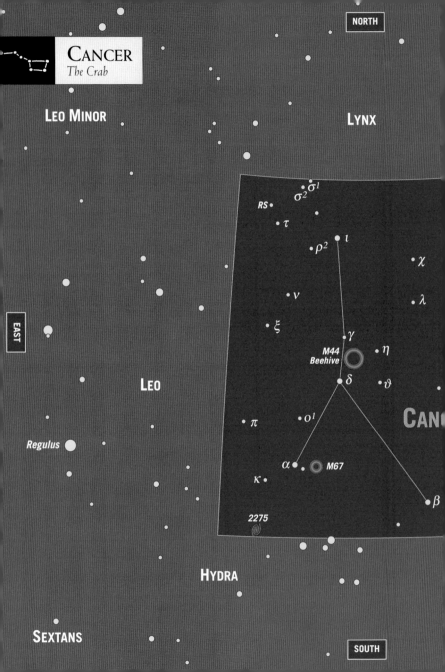

NORTH

CANCER
The Crab

LEO MINOR

LYNX

σ^2 σ^1

RS

τ

ρ^2 ι

χ

λ

ν

ξ

γ

η

M44
Beehive

δ

ϑ

EAST

LEO

CANC

π

o^1

Regulus

α

M67

κ

β

2275

HYDRA

SEXTANS

SOUTH

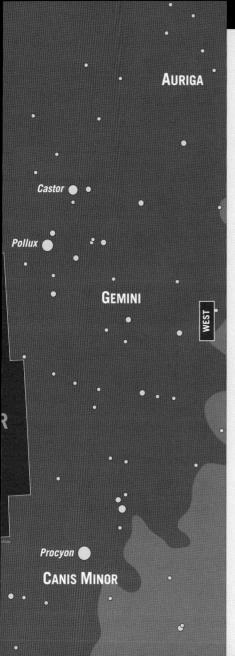

AURIGA

Castor

Pollux

GEMINI

WEST

Procyon

CANIS MINOR

MYTHOLOGY: The constellation Cancer is named for a crab that was sent to bite Hercules while he fought Hydra, a many-headed serpent who grew two heads each time one was cut off. Hercules stepped on the crab and killed it.

DESCRIPTION: Cancer is an ancient constellation, recognized thousands of years ago by the Greeks and Romans, who knew that on the longest day of the year, the sun was in Cancer. It is a faint constellation that lies along the ecliptic and is part of the zodiac, the band of constellations through which the planets travel. It looks nothing like a crab. The constellation's most notable feature is the Beehive star cluster, also known as the Praesepe cluster and as M44.

VIEWING TIPS: Cancer, visible in our evening sky in winter and spring, is nestled between Leo to the east and Gemini to the west. Using the spring or winter sky map, find these two constellations to pick out Cancer.

BEST VIEWING TIME: February and March.

SEASON MAPS: Spring, winter.

91

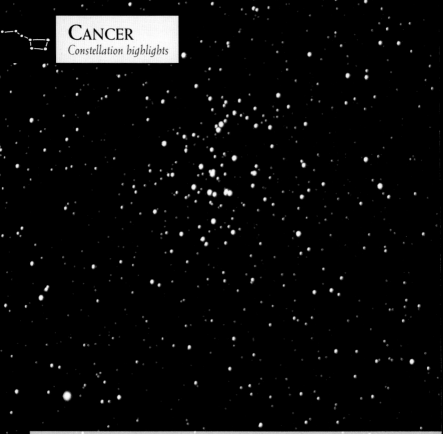

Within the dim constellation of Cancer is an open star cluster that can easily be seen with the naked eye. It has three names: its ancient name Praesepe, which means the Manger; the Beehive, because its stars look like a swarm of bees; and M44, its name in the Messier Catalog. Cancer has another notable star cluster called M67.

DESCRIPTION: The Beehive (on the left side of this photograph) is one of the brightest open star clusters in the sky, with a magnitude of 3.1. At only 520 light-years away, it is also one of the closest. The Beehive spreads over a large area, about three times the area of the full moon. Its brightest single star is of magnitude 6.3.

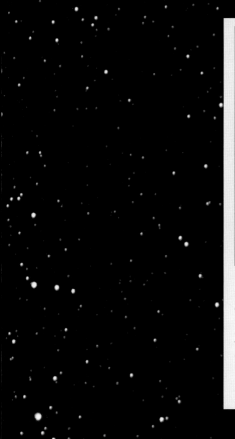

STAR CLUSTER M67

DESCRIPTION: Open star cluster M67 is more challenging to see than the Beehive. At 3.2 billion years of age, it is one of the oldest open star clusters known. **VIEWING TIPS:** M67, at magnitude 6.9, is too faint to spot with the naked eye. With binoculars it can be found in all but the most light-polluted skies, 8° (about one fist) south of the Beehive and a little bit east.

VIEWING TIPS: Right smack in the middle of Cancer, the Beehive can be found by finding the midpoint between Regulus, the bright star in Leo, and Castor and Pollux, Gemini's twin stars. The Beehive is a good object to look at with the averted vision technique. Find the general area of the Beehive in the sky, and then look just to the side of it. Its light will then fall on a part of your eye that's not "tired," and you'll find it easier to see than you would if you looked straight at it. Binoculars, held steady, provide an impressive view of the 75 readily visible stars of this cluster.

SEASON MAPS: Spring, winter.

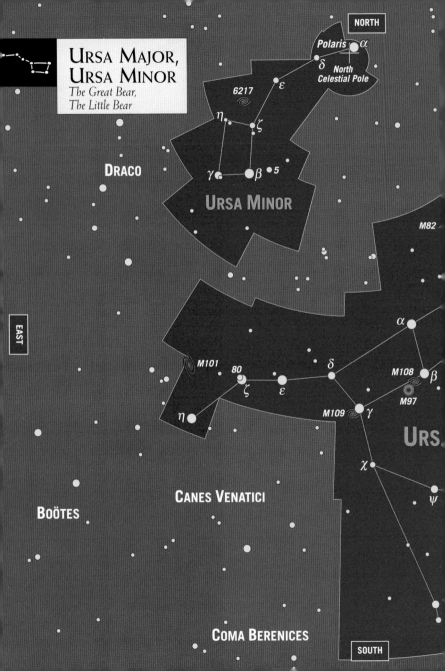

URSA MAJOR, URSA MINOR
The Great Bear,
The Little Bear

Polaris α
δ North
Celestial Pole

6217
η ζ ε
γ β 5

URSA MINOR

DRACO

M82

EAST

α

M101
80 δ M108 β
ζ ε M97
η M109 γ M97
χ URS.
ψ

CANES VENATICI

BOÖTES

COMA BERENICES

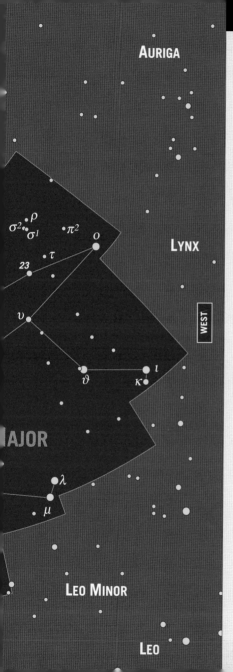

AURIGA

σ² ρ
σ¹ • π²
23 τ
o
LYNX
υ
ϑ κ¹ ι
MAJOR
λ
μ
LEO MINOR
LEO

WEST

MYTHOLOGY: Ursa Major, the Great Bear, is sometimes said to have been a maiden turned into a bear and placed in the sky by the god Zeus's jealous wife. The bear's cub, Ursa Minor, the Little Bear, was placed there with her.

DESCRIPTION: The Big Dipper, part of the constellation Ursa Major, and the Little Dipper, another name for Ursa Minor, are among the most familiar patterns in the sky. They are circumpolar, which means they revolve around the north celestial pole (Polaris, the North Star, marks the pole) and are visible from most northern latitudes every night of the year.

VIEWING TIPS: The dippers appear in different positions throughout the year. Sometimes the Big Dipper sits like a pot on a stove; at other times it's upside down. Find the Big Dipper, then draw a line north from the pointers, the two stars at the bowl's end (the alpha α and beta β stars). You will come directly to Polaris, at the end of the Little Dipper's handle.

BEST VIEWING TIME: Ursa Major: February to May; Ursa Minor: May to June.

SEASON MAPS: All.

95

Many of Ursa Major's stars lie only 60 to 80 light-years away and may be part of a loose star cluster. Those that form the Big Dipper (pictured here) are the brightest members.

DESCRIPTION: The Big Dipper looks like a huge ladle lying across the sky. It is only a small part of the constellation Ursa Major, but is one of the brightest and most recognizable shapes in the night sky. The dipper forms the bear's hind end and its long tail. The bear's other stars, forming the forequarters and legs, are less bright.

MIZAR AND ALCOR

DESCRIPTION: The middle star (zeta ζ) in the Big Dipper's handle, at the crook, is actually two stars: Mizar (Arabic for horse) and Alcor (the rider). Mizar is a bright, white star of magnitude 2.2. Alcor is of magnitude 4, and may not be visible in city skies. **VIEWING TIPS:** Try your binoculars on this attractive pair. Mizar offers a further treat to viewers with a telescope: It is actually a pair of two equally bright stars.

GALAXIES M81 AND M82

DESCRIPTION: M81 (on the left in the photograph) and M82 are a pair of galaxies that lie about 12 million light-years away. M81 is a spiral galaxy, like the Milky Way; M82 is an irregular galaxy. **VIEWING TIPS:** Point your binoculars directly north of the front half of the bear to find M81. You won't be able to see the spiral pattern, but at magnitude 6.9, it is one of the brightest spirals in the sky. You need a telescope to see M82.

VIEWING TIPS: Ursa Major is close to the north celestial pole, which means it is a circumpolar constellation, visible in the northern sky all year long. Look at the seasonal maps to see its position in the sky in each season.

SEASON MAPS: All.

97

URSA MAJOR AND URSA MINOR

The Little Dipper shape of Ursa Minor is not as bright as the Big Dipper, but its pattern is clear. Its alpha (α) star, Polaris, is called the North Star because of its position, at the celestial pole.

DESCRIPTION: At the end of the Little Dipper's handle is the North Star, Polaris. The North Star marks the north celestial pole, which is the extension of Earth's north pole in space. As Earth turns, the entire sky seems to rotate around this point. Polaris is the brightest star in the constellation, with a magnitude of only 2.

VIEWING TIPS: Polaris is in the sky at northern latitudes all year long. The pointer stars at the end of the Big Dipper's bowl point to Polaris.

SEASON MAPS: All.

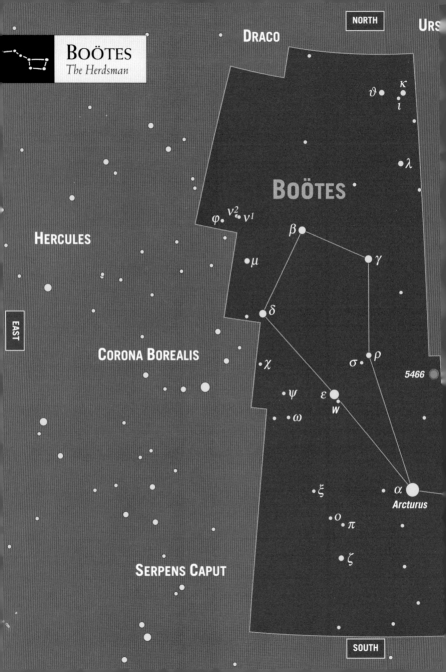

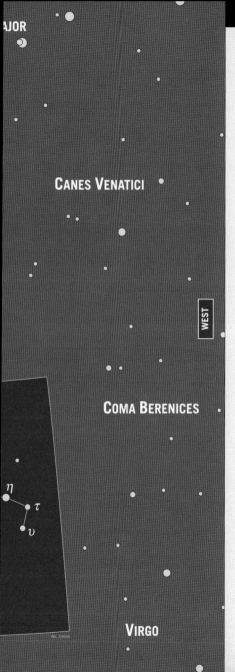

MYTHOLOGY: Boötes is usually called the Herdsman and is said to have been the son of the god Jupiter. Some legends say he invented the plow, and was placed in the sky near the Big Dipper, which is sometimes called the Plow. In other legends he is known as the Bear Keeper and is said to be herding Ursa Major and Ursa Minor, the Great and Little Bears, around the north celestial pole.

DESCRIPTION: The constellation of Boötes (pronounced bo-OH-tease) has the shape of a kite or an ice-cream cone. Its bright red giant star Arcturus, the alpha (α) star, is at the bottom of the kite (or the cone).

VIEWING TIPS: Boötes is south and a bit east of Ursa Major (follow the arc of the Dipper's handle to reach Arcturus) and north of Virgo (continue the arc down from Arcturus and you will find Virgo's bright star, Spica). If you watch the sky off and on for a few hours, you will see how Boötes appears to follow the Great Bear around the sky.

BEST VIEWING TIME: May to July.

SEASON MAPS: Spring, summer.

BOÖTES
Constellation highlights

The kite shape of Boötes extends up from the bright star Arcturus, which lies only 36 light-years from Earth.

DESCRIPTION: Arcturus, Boötes' alpha (α) star, is 20 times larger than the sun. It is the brightest red giant in the sky and, at −0.05 magnitude, the fourth brightest of all stars. To the naked eye it has a yellow-orange tint. Izar (epsilon ε), which to the naked eye appears to be a 2.5 magnitude single star, is actually a triple star.

VIEWING TIPS: Look at Arcturus through binoculars to make the color really leap out. If you have a small telescope, you should be able to see two of Izar's three stars: a red giant and a bluish white star. Izar lies 10° (about one fist) northeast of Arcturus. In this photograph, Arcturus is the bright star at the bottom, with the stars marking the kite (including Izar) extending up to the left.

SEASON MAPS: Spring, summer.

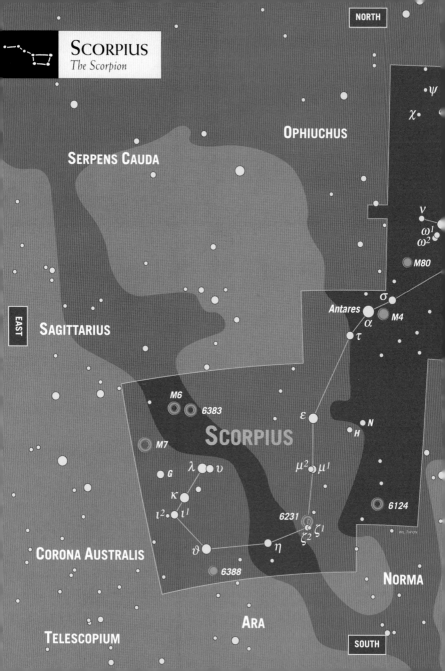

LIBRA

WEST

HYDRA

CENTAURUS

LUPUS

SCORPIUS

MYTHOLOGY: According to legend, the constellation Scorpius was placed in the sky in honor of the tiny scorpion that stung and killed the boastful hunter Orion. The two enemies are never seen in the sky at the same time.

DESCRIPTION: With its curving body, its claws, and its whiplike tail, Scorpius is one of those special few constellations that actually look like the thing they were named for. It has a bright red alpha (α) star in the center, called Antares, a red supergiant that is one of the few visible stars that has a reasonable probability of turning into a supernova in the next million years. Scorpius lies in an interesting region of the sky where the zodiac and the Milky Way intersect. It has many star clusters and nebulas.

VIEWING TIPS: Look for Scorpius along the zodiac between Sagittarius and Ophiuchus to the east and Libra to the west. The Antares region and the band of Milky Way behind the tail are interesting areas to observe with binoculars.

BEST VIEWING TIME: June to August.

SEASON MAPS: Summer.

ANTARES

With its interesting shape, its brilliant reddish star Antares, and the Milky Way Galaxy lying behind the stars of its tail, Scorpius is a fascinating area of the sky.

DESCRIPTION: Antares, the alpha (α) star, is a bright (1.1 magnitude) orange-red supergiant about 600 light-years away. It lies in a region of the Milky Way full of glowing nebulas in which new stars are forming. Near the scorpion's tail are M7, a bright, 220-million-year-old open star cluster lying about 780 light-years away; and M6, a similar but more distant (1,900 light-years) open cluster.

VIEWING TIPS: Find Scorpius in the summer sky by looking south and fairly low (near the horizon). Antares lies where the scorpion's heart might be. Look between the triangle of stars at the end of the scorpion's tail and the spout of the teapot of Sagittarius for a fuzzy patch. This is M7, covering an area the size of two full moons. Look northwest from M7 to find M6. It will be more of a challenge, depending on local conditions.

SEASON MAPS: Summer.

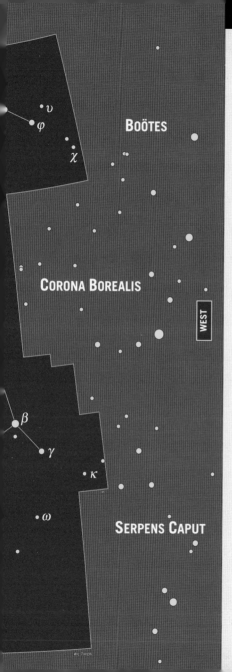

BOÖTES

CORONA BOREALIS

WEST

SERPENS CAPUT

υ
φ
χ
β
γ
κ
ω

WIL TIRION

HERCULES

MYTHOLOGY: Hercules is the famous strongman who had to perform Twelve Labors in order to break free of slavery. He killed the lion now seen in the sky as the constellation Leo, the many-headed serpent that forms the constellation Hydra, and the dragon that winds through the sky as the constellation Draco.

DESCRIPTION: Hercules is a rather unremarkable area of the sky. Its stars are mainly of magnitude 3 to 4. You may be able to pick out the figure of a man here, although he is kneeling and upside down. It is easier to see a shape in the center of the constellation called the Keystone.

VIEWING TIPS: Hercules lies between the brilliant bluish-white star Vega (constellation Lyra) and the brilliant orange-red star Arcturus (constellation Boötes). Between these two bright stars sits the Keystone, a crooked square formed by Hercules' epsilon (ε), zeta (ζ), eta (η), and pi (π) stars. Hercules' head, marked by the alpha (α) star, Ras Algethi, lies near the Milky Way.

BEST VIEWING TIME: June and July.

SEASON MAPS: Spring, summer, fall.

Hercules is very large but has no really bright stars. Its most recognizable part is the four-star Keystone, pictured here.

DESCRIPTION: Ras Algethi (ras-awl-JEE-thee), a red supergiant star, marks Hercules' head. Its name comes from Arabic and means "the kneeler's head." The constellation's highlight is the globular cluster M13, also called the Hercules Cluster. It is the most impressive globular cluster visible in the northern sky.

VIEWING TIPS: Trace a line from the bright star Vega (constellation Lyra, to the east), to the red giant Arcturus (constellation Boötes), to find Hercules' Keystone, right in between. M13 lies along the west side of the Keystone. Ras Algethi lies to the south of the Keystone. You may be able to see this star's orange-red color with binoculars. In a small telescope you can see that it is a double star, with a yellow giant companion. The red star varies in brightness, and the pair's magnitude varies from 2.8 to 3.8.

SEASON MAPS: Spring, summer, fall.

GLOBULAR CLUSTER M13

DESCRIPTION: At 23,400 light-years away, this huge cluster of roughly 300,000 stars appears as a fuzzy star about half the width of the full moon. It has a magnitude of 5.9. **VIEWING TIPS:** To the naked eye M13 is a faint patch of light. Look through binoculars or a small telescope to see it more clearly. You need a large telescope to see the cluster's individual stars.

GLOBULAR CLUSTER M92

DESCRIPTION: For more of a challenge, get your binoculars and look for M92, another globular cluster. It is a bit fainter than M13, at a magnitude of 6.5, and lies 25,000 light-years from Earth. **VIEWING TIPS:** M92 lies north of the Keystone, not far west of Vega.

111

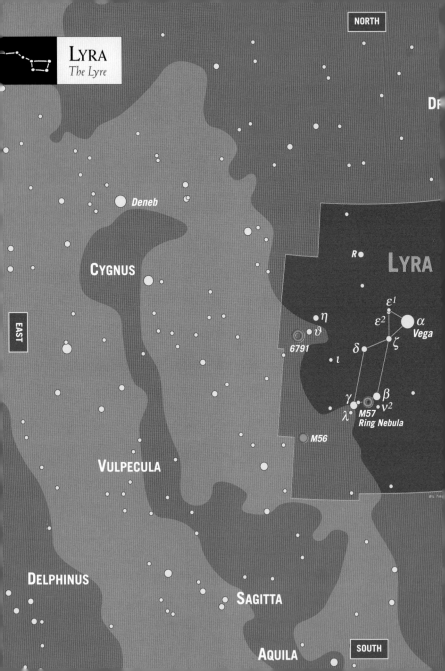

NORTH

LYRA
The Lyre

Deneb

CYGNUS

EAST

DF

R

LYRA

ε^1

ε^2

α
Vega

η

ϑ

δ

ζ

6791

ι

γ

β

λ

ν^2

M57
Ring Nebula

M56

VULPECULA

DELPHINUS

SAGITTA

AQUILA

SOUTH

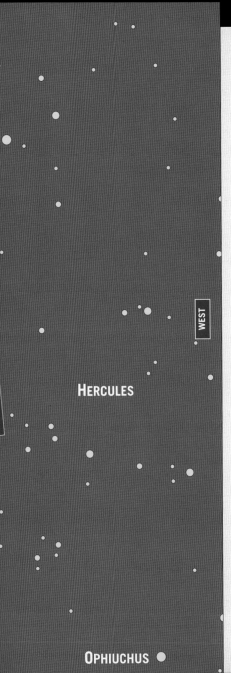

HERCULES

WEST

OPHIUCHUS

LYRA

MYTHOLOGY: Lyra represents the lyre, an instrument like a harp, that Orpheus, son of the god Apollo, played to bring his beloved bride back from the underworld.

DESCRIPTION: Lyra is a small but striking constellation consisting of a tiny triangle attached to a parallelogram (a rectangle leaning over). In the triangle lies one of the brightest and most colorful stars in the night sky: the blue-white star Vega. The epsilon (ϵ) and zeta (ζ) stars mark the other two corners of the triangle. Zeta is also part of the parallelogram representing the lyre.

VIEWING TIPS: Immediately east of Hercules, Lyra is a highlight of the summer sky. Vega (the alpha α star) marks the brightest corner of the summer triangle; Altair (the alpha α star in Aquila) and Deneb (the alpha α star in Cygnus) mark the other corners. As night falls in summer, this large triangle is the first star pattern to appear. In mid-August, Vega is almost directly overhead in much of North America.

BEST VIEWING TIME: July to August.

SEASON MAPS: Spring, summer, fall.

LYRA
Constellation highlights

The small constellation of Lyra is one of the beauties of the summer sky. Diamondlike Vega is the fifth brightest star of all.

DESCRIPTION: Vega, Lyra's alpha (α) star, is part of the large Summer Triangle, along with the alpha stars of the constellations Cygnus and Aquila. The epsilon (ε) star, called epsilon Lyrae, is a well-known "double-double" star. To the naked eye, it appears as a single star of magnitude 4. Through binoculars, held rock-steady, two white stars of equal brightness become clear. With a small telescope, you can see that each star is itself a close double star.

VIEWING TIPS: Look overhead on summer nights for the Summer Triangle. Vega marks the western corner.

SEASON MAPS: Spring, summer, fall.

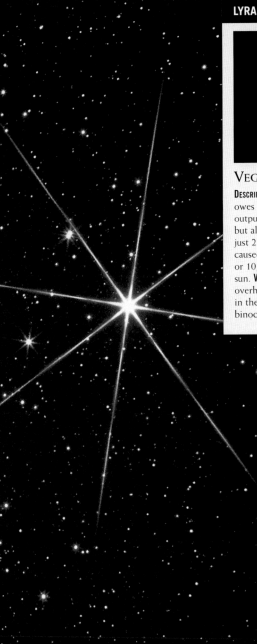

VEGA

DESCRIPTION: Vega has a magnitude of 0. It owes its brightness not only to its energy output (about 52 times that of our sun), but also to its relative nearness to Earth, at just 25 light-years. Its bluish-white color is caused by its high temperature (18,000°F or 10,000°C), almost twice as hot as our sun. **VIEWING TIPS:** Vega shines almost directly overhead on summer and early fall nights in the Northern Hemisphere. Use binoculars to see its color more clearly.

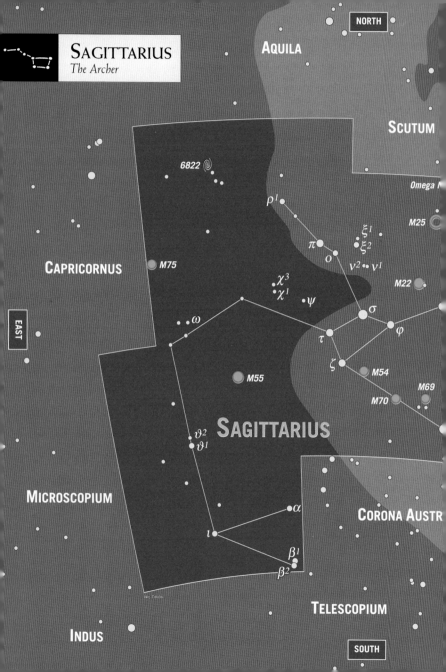

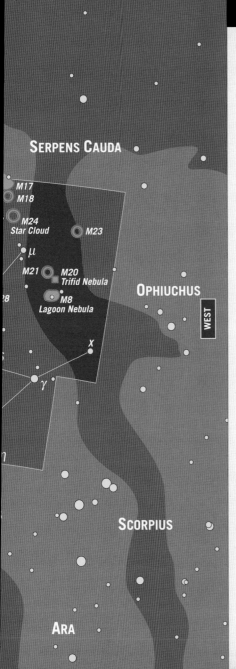

MYTHOLOGY: Sagittarius, the Archer, is a centaur—a mythological creature with the four legs and body of a horse and the head and arms of a man. He is holding a bow and arrow, aimed at Scorpius, the Scorpion.

DESCRIPTION: The constellation of Sagittarius bears little resemblance to a centaur with a bow and arrow. Most people, however, can pick out the shape of a teapot, in the western half of the constellation. Sagittarius is one of the most studied regions of the night sky. As one of the zodiacal constellations, it often is visited by one or more planets. But its greater interest is in its location: It lies in the direction of our galaxy's center. When we look toward the center we can see masses of stars, star clusters, and nebulas.

VIEWING TIPS: Sagittarius doesn't get very high in the sky at northern latitudes. It sits fairly low toward the south in summer, east of Scorpius.

BEST VIEWING TIME: July to August.

SEASON MAPS: Summer.

SAGITTARIUS
Constellation highlights

Our solar system is located toward the outside of the Milky Way Galaxy's spiral disk. Sagittarius lies between Earth and the center of the galaxy. When we look toward this constellation we see the interior of our galaxy from the side, and the Milky Way appears as a cloudy band. (Hold up a plate and look at it from the side to get an idea of Earth's viewpoint of the galaxy.).

DESCRIPTION: The brightest stars of Sagittarius trace the outline of a teapot (lower left quarter of this photograph). Within the cloudy streak that forms the backdrop for this constellation are many nebulas, star clusters, and stars. The Lagoon (M8), Trifid (M20), and Omega (M17) nebulas are just three of the fascinating gas and dust clouds in this area.

VIEWING TIPS: You can see the Milky Way in Sagittarius with the naked eye. The longer you look, the more you will see, as your eyes become adjusted to the darkness. It is a fun area to scan with binoculars. Follow up with a small telescope, zooming in on the many nebulas and star clusters.

SEASON MAPS: Summer.

GLOBULAR CLUSTER M22

DESCRIPTION: Sagittarius is noted for its large number of star clusters. Globular cluster M22, at magnitude 5.2, is among the brighter globular clusters in our sky. It lies 10,000 light-years from Earth. **VIEWING TIPS:** M22 is northeast of the top of the teapot. Binoculars will give you a sweeping view of M22 in the midst of all the stars and objects around it. A telescope will bring out its details nicely, allowing you to see the cluster's individual stars.

LAGOON NEBULA

DESCRIPTION: The most notable of a number of interesting objects in Sagittarius is M8, the Lagoon Nebula. This is the largest of the bright nebulas in our sky, stretching about four times the area of the disk of the moon. **VIEWING TIPS:** The Lagoon Nebula is large but not very bright. It is invisible to the naked eye under most conditions. You can see it with binoculars, particularly on dark moonless nights. Give your eyes time to adjust to the darkness.

MYTHOLOGY: According to a Greek legend, the god Zeus turned himself into a swan, represented in the sky by Cygnus. The swan is said to be the father of Leda's son Pollux, one of the twin stars of the constellation Gemini.

DESCRIPTION: Cygnus, the Swan, is also known as the Northern Cross. The colorful double star Albireo (beta β) marks the head of the swan and the bottom of the cross. The constellation lies right along the Milky Way. It has several open clusters and nebulas, including the North America Nebula.

VIEWING TIPS: Cygnus flies high across the summer and autumn sky, heading southwestward. Its alpha (α) star, Deneb, marks one corner of the Summer Triangle; the other corners are marked by Vega (constellation Lyra) and Altair (constellation Aquila).

BEST VIEWING TIME: July to September.

SEASON MAPS: Spring, summer, fall.

CYGNUS
Constellation highlights

Cygnus, the Swan, is a large and bright constellation that actually looks like its namesake. Set against the background of the Milky Way, it is an area rich in nebulas, stars, and star clusters.

DESCRIPTION: Deneb, the alpha (α) star, is a bluish-white supergiant of magnitude 1.5. It marks the Swan's tail. The beta (β) star, Albireo, is a double star marking the Swan's head. M39 is an open star cluster about 900 light-years away.

VIEWING TIPS: Cygnus is high in the sky in late summer. The bright stars of the cross are readily visible. Try your binoculars on M39 (northeast of Deneb); it's not very dense, but binoculars should bring it out nicely.

SEASON MAPS: Spring, summer, fall.

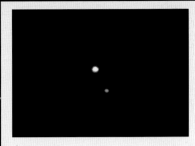

ALBIREO

DESCRIPTION: One of the best-known double stars in the sky, Albireo has two bright, colorful, well-separated components. The brighter star is an orange-colored giant star of magnitude 3.1. The other is a blue main sequence star of magnitude 5.1.
VIEWING TIPS: This very pretty pair is well worth a look at through a small telescope. To the naked eye it looks like a single star with a magnitude of 3.

NORTH AMERICA NEBULA

DESCRIPTION: Like most constellations in the Milky Way, Cygnus is rich in nebulas. One, located a few degrees east of Deneb, is called the North America Nebula (or NGC 7000), because of its resemblance to that continent. The nebula's red coloring is from an abundance of hydrogen atoms, which glow when they are energized. Nearby is the Pelican Nebula (IC 5067), which also got its name from its shape.
VIEWING TIPS: These two nebulas are faint, and require a telescope to be seen.

123

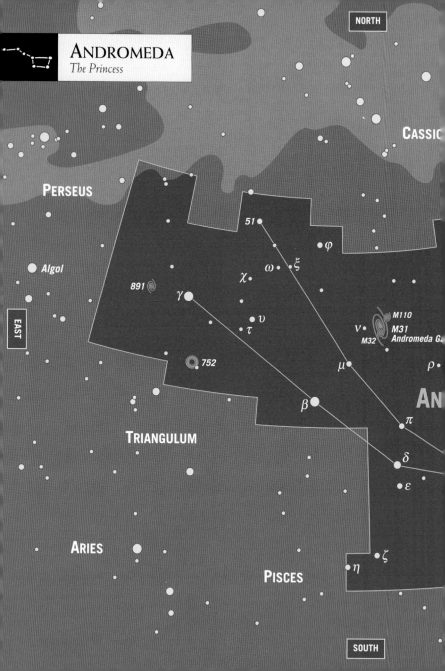

NORTH

ANDROMEDA
The Princess

CASSIC

PERSEUS

Algol

891

γ

51

φ

ω ξ

χ

υ

τ

752

β

TRIANGULUM

ARIES

PISCES

η ζ

EAST

ν

M110
M31
Andromeda Ga
M32

ρ

AN

π

δ

ε

SOUTH

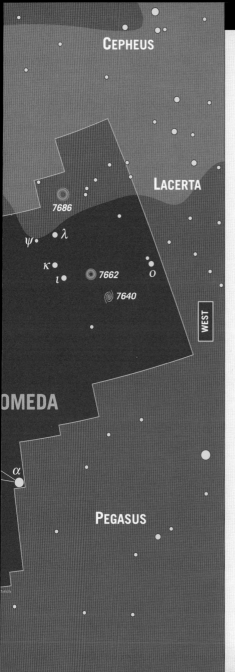

CEPHEUS

LACERTA

7686

ψ λ

κ
ι 7662 o

7640

WEST

OMEDA

α

PEGASUS

ANDROMEDA

MYTHOLOGY: Andromeda was the princess daughter of Queen Cassiopeia and King Cepheus. She was chained to a cliff to be sacrificed to the sea monster Cetus, but was rescued by Perseus, the Hero. Every one of these characters is commemorated in a constellation.

DESCRIPTION: Andromeda is a long, thin, V shape, with the alpha (α) star, called Alpheratz, marking the spot where the two sides meet. Alpheratz also forms one corner of the Great Square of Pegasus. When we look toward Andromeda we are looking away from our galaxy's center and out into deep space. More than 2 million light-years away in that direction lies another galaxy, the Andromeda Galaxy (M31).

VIEWING TIPS: Andromeda is immediately south of Cassiopeia, the easy-to-find W-shaped constellation. Cassiopeia is a circumpolar constellation, visible in the northern sky all year.

BEST VIEWING TIME: September to November.

SEASON MAPS: Summer, fall, winter.

ANDROMEDA
Constellation highlights

The stars that we can see with the naked eye are within our region of the Milky Way Galaxy. The constellation Andromeda offers us a window out of our own galaxy—and a glimpse at another.

DESCRIPTION: Look carefully for the stars of Andromeda. They will lead you to the Great Galaxy of Andromeda, also called the Andromeda Galaxy or M31.

VIEWING TIPS: Use the Andromeda constellation map to find Alpheratz, the 2.1 magnitude alpha (α) star at the point of the V shape. Trace up the V to the second pair of stars (mu μ and bright beta β). Using your fingers, measure off the distance between the two stars of that second pair. Then measure northwest of the mu star the same distance. The galaxy's nucleus appears to the naked eye as a fuzzy patch of light. In this picture, Alpheratz is at bottom right, beta is the bright star at left center; mu and the Andromeda Galaxy are to the upper right of beta.

SEASON MAPS: Summer, fall, winter.

ANDROMEDA GALAXY

DESCRIPTION: The Andromeda Galaxy is the nearest spiral galaxy to ours—2.5 million light-years away. It belongs to the same galaxy cluster as the Milky Way, called the Local Group. **VIEWING TIPS:** The Andromeda Galaxy is the most distant object the unaided human eye can see. It appears as a faint oval of light. Urban light pollution can drown it out. Through binoculars the disk of the galaxy shows more clearly and is much brighter.

ELLIPTICAL GALAXY M32

DESCRIPTION: The Andromeda Galaxy has a small companion galaxy called M32. It is a dwarf elliptical galaxy. In the picture of the Andromeda Galaxy at the top of this page, M32 is the bright spot to the upper left. Another nearby galaxy, M110, is the larger spot at the lower right. **VIEWING TIPS:** M32 is of 8th magnitude and can be seen only with a telescope.

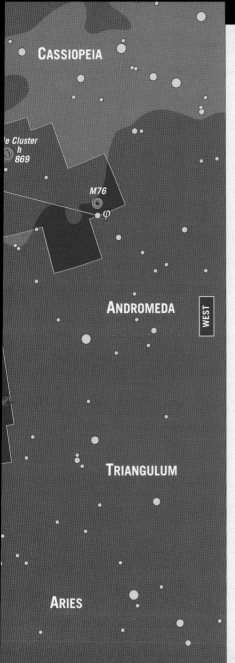

CASSIOPEIA

le Cluster
h
869

M76

φ

ANDROMEDA

WEST

TRIANGULUM

ARIES

PERSEUS

MYTHOLOGY: The hero for whom this constellation is named saved Princess Andromeda, daughter of Queen Cassiopeia and King Cepheus, from the sea monster Cetus. Perseus also cut off the head of Medusa, a monster with snakes for hair. When he held her head aloft in the sea, Pegasus, the Winged Horse, was born from the sea foam.

DESCRIPTION: The constellation Perseus doesn't look much like a hero holding the head of Medusa, but it does lie along the Milky Way and is full of interesting sights. This constellation's most attractive features are its bright beta (β) star, Algol, which varies its light output, and the attractive Double Cluster, a pair of bright, open star clusters.

VIEWING TIPS: Perseus lies north of Taurus, east of Andromeda, and west of Auriga, the Charioteer, which is distinguished by Capella, the 7th brightest star in the sky. Perseus's alpha (α) star, Mirphak (magnitude 1.8), lies at the center of the constellation.

BEST VIEWING TIME: November to January.

SEASON MAPS: Spring, fall, winter.

PERSEUS
Constellation highlights

A highlight of the constellation Perseus is the beta (β) star, Algol. Perseus, the Hero, is usually pictured holding the head of Medusa. Algol represents Medusa's eye and is nicknamed the Demon Star.

DESCRIPTION: Algol is a special kind of star called an "eclipsing binary" that appears to "blink," or go from bright to dim to bright again over a period of time. Algol is actually a pair of stars that pass one another in their orbits. The brighter star in the pair is a large, hot star of 2.1 magnitude. The other member of the pair is even larger, though cooler. About every three days the cooler star passes in front of the brighter star, and the pair's magnitude dims to 3.3 for about 10 hours—and Medusa appears to blink. Then the bright star emerges and the magnitude rises again.

VIEWING TIPS: Algol is an interesting object to look at over a period of time. Find the star in the sky for several nights in a row. See if you can tell when the eclipse has occurred.

SEASON MAPS: Spring, fall, winter.

ALGOL

DESCRIPTION: The bright star of Algol's pair is eclipsed by the cooler, dimmer star about every three days. **VIEWING TIPS:** Compare Algol's brightness with the brightness of neighboring stars. Make notes of which are brighter, dimmer, and of equal brightness. By making such notes over several nights you should be able to tell when Algol "blinked."

DOUBLE CLUSTER

DESCRIPTION: North of Algol, between it and the constellation Cassiopeia, is a pair of open star clusters called the Double Cluster (or h and chi χ Persei, or NGC 869 and 884). **VIEWING TIPS:** These clusters, 7,000 light-years away, are faintly visible to the unaided eye; light pollution can easily wipe them out. Binoculars bring out this pair of clusters nicely.

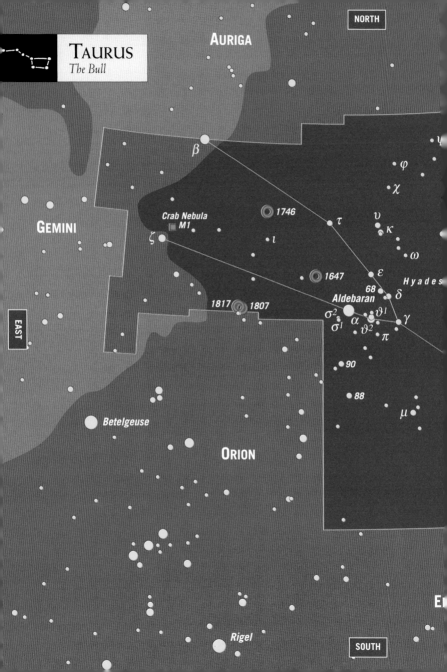

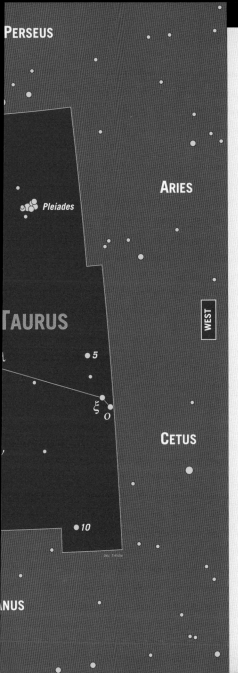

PERSEUS

ARIES

Pleiades

TAURUS

WEST

5

ξ
Ο

CETUS

10

WIL TIRION

NUS

TAURUS

MYTHOLOGY: In myths from cultures the world over, Taurus represents a bull. In a Greek legend, the god Zeus transformed himself into a white bull, kidnapped the princess Europa, and swam to the Greek island of Crete with her on his back.

DESCRIPTION: Taurus is one of the highlights of the winter sky. It is usually depicted as just the front end of a bull, with the alpha (α) star (Aldebaran) and the epsilon (ε) star marking the eyes and the beta (β) and zeta (ζ) stars at the tips of the horns. Taurus is home to two of the loveliest star clusters in the sky: the Pleiades, or Seven Sisters, and the Hyades.

VIEWING TIPS: Taurus is high in the sky in winter. Follow the stars of Orion's belt northwestward, and you can't miss it. The stars of the Hyades swarm around Aldebaran on the bull's face. The stars of the Pleiades sit on the bull's back. At the tip of the bull's eastern horn lies the Crab Nebula, a remnant from a supernova that exploded in the year 1054.

BEST VIEWING TIME: December to February.

SEASON MAPS: Fall, winter.

The stars of the Pleiades (PLEE-uh-deeze) represent seven sisters—the daughters of Atlas and Pleione—who went to Zeus for help when they couldn't shake off a persistent suitor, Orion. Zeus turned them into stars in the sky, and there they remain, just out of Orion's reach.

DESCRIPTION: The Pleiades (also called M45) is an open cluster of hundreds of stars 410 light-years from Earth. The Greeks called this group the Seven Sisters, but with so much light pollution dimming views of the night sky today, most people can see only five or six stars with the naked eye. The seven brightest stars of the cluster range in magnitude from 3 to 6. In this photograph of Taurus, the Pleiades is to the right, Aldebaran and the Hyades are at bottom center, and beta (β) is to the left.

VIEWING TIPS: Trace the three stars of Orion's belt northwestward past Taurus's bright orange star Aldebaran; you'll come straight to the Pleiades, a misty, delicate-looking collection of stars.

SEASON MAPS: Fall, winter.

PLEIADES

DESCRIPTION: The Pleiades is a young cluster, at 100 million years, and new stars are still forming within its clouds of gas and dust.
VIEWING TIPS: The big, massive, hot stars of the cluster are visible to the naked eye. Many of the less massive, smaller, and cooler stars are visible through binoculars or a small telescope.

TAURUS
Constellation highlights

Taurus is a constellation full of surprises. The Pleiades is the most famous star cluster in the sky, but another group of sisters (the half sisters of the Pleiades) resides here as well: the Hyades.

DESCRIPTION: The Hyades star cluster is closer, and therefore looks larger than the Pleiades. It makes up most of the V shape that marks the face of the bull. The very brightest star in the V is one of the major attention-grabbers of the night sky—the bright orange-red giant Aldebaran, a 1st magnitude star. In spite of its location, Aldebaran is not actually a member of the Hyades; it just happens to lie along our line of sight to the cluster. The Hyades is located only 150 light-years from Earth, but Aldebaran is even closer, at just 65 light-years. The Hyades has been an important object of study for astronomers, who have learned things about stars, star clusters, the evolution of the Milky Way Galaxy, and even about measuring distances in the universe by observing it. The Hyades cluster is old enough, at about 660 million years, for some of its hot blue stars to have evolved to the red giant and supergiant stages.

VIEWING TIPS: The stars of Orion's belt point almost directly to Aldebaran. With binoculars or a small, low-power telescope, look for color variation among the Hyades cluster's brightest stars (they are much more colorful than the younger Pleiades, which are all main sequence stars).

SEASON MAPS: Fall, winter.

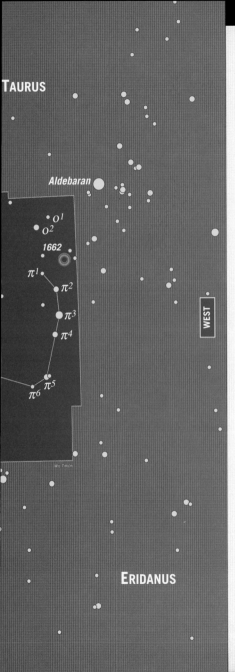

TAURUS

Aldebaran

O¹
O²

1662

π^1
π^2
π^3
π^4
π^5
π^6

WILL TIRION

WEST

ERIDANUS

MYTHOLOGY: In one myth, Artemis, the goddess of the moon and the hunt, fell in love with Orion. Sadly, she accidentally killed him. She placed him in the sky, marked with bright stars, but has kept the moon cold and lifeless ever since.

DESCRIPTION: Orion is on the celestial equator and so is visible from both the Northern and Southern Hemispheres. The red star Betelgeuse (alpha α) marks one shoulder, the star Bellatrix (gamma γ) marks the other. Rigel (beta β) and Saiph (kappa κ) mark the knees. Three stars in a row form Orion's belt; hanging from the belt is his sword. He holds a shield in one hand (to keep Taurus, the Bull, from charging him) and a club in the other. Orion is notable for its pattern, its bright and colorful stars, and the interesting nebulas that swirl around the lower half.

VIEWING TIPS: Orion is easy to find in the winter sky: The three belt stars are unmistakable. In fall it starts to rise low in the eastern sky and by spring has disappeared over the western horizon.

BEST VIEWING TIME: January to February.

SEASON MAPS: Fall, winter.

139

The finest constellation in the sky, Orion attracts amateur and professional astronomers alike. It looks something like its namesake, the Hunter, and is bright with fascinating stars.

DESCRIPTION: You should easily be able to see the reddish color of the star Betelgeuse (BET-el-jooze). At 0.5 magnitude, Betelgeuse is the brightest red supergiant in the sky, edging out Antares (1.1 magnitude) in Scorpius. Its distance is estimated at around 430 light-years. This is much closer than the 1,500 light-year distance of many of the other bright objects in Orion. Although identified as Orion's alpha (α) star, Betelgeuse is actually a bit fainter than the beta (β) star, Rigel (RYE-jil), which has a magnitude of 0. Rigel is a hot, blue supergiant that lies about 800 light-years away.

VIEWING TIPS: Betelgeuse and Rigel are Orion's brightest stars. When you look up, Betelgeuse is the pale orange star marking the left (eastern) shoulder, and Rigel is the blue-white star at the right knee.

SEASON MAPS: Fall, winter.

BETELGEUSE

DESCRIPTION: Betelgeuse is a variable star, which means its magnitude brightens and dims rather than holding steady. The star is nearing the end of its lifetime, and is actively blowing away much of its mass in preparation for its climactic ending as a supernova sometime within the coming million years. **VIEWING TIPS:** This Hubble Space Telescope image shows cloud buildup around Betelgeuse. From Earth we see a slightly reddish star.

RIGEL

DESCRIPTION: Blue supergiants are smaller than red supergiants. While blue Rigel is about 50 times larger than our sun, red Betelgeuse is an astounding 400 times larger. Rigel, however, is a far hotter star, with a temperature of about 18,000°F (10,000°C), compared to Betelgeuse's 4,500°F (2,500°C). **VIEWING TIPS:** It is difficult for our eyes to pick up star colors. Rigel and Betelgeuse help bring out each other's colors by contrast.

ORION
Constellation highlights

Orion not only has fascinating stars, but also has many nebulas in which new stars (and possibly planets) are forming. The Orion Nebula is the centerpiece of the Orion star-forming region.

DESCRIPTION: Clouds of gas and dust run throughout Orion. In the Orion Nebula (or M42), pictured here, these clouds are brightened by an extremely luminous star in a group of four stars called the Trapezium. These young stars, only a few hundred thousand years old, are hot, large, and luminous. The hottest and brightest one puts out huge quantities of ultraviolet light, energizing the surrounding gases and causing them to glow. This photograph shows the glowing nebula.

VIEWING TIPS: The Orion Nebula, 1,500 light-years away, is bright enough to appear as a smudge of brightness in the middle of Orion's sword (which hangs down from the belt). This nebula is a must-see with binoculars.

SEASON MAPS: Fall, winter.

TRAPEZIUM

DESCRIPTION: This is a closeup of the nebula lit up by the Trapezium stars. Within the nebula, new stars are in the making. In another million years or so, there will be another star cluster in our sky, appearing very bright and compact. **VIEWING TIPS:** A small telescope brings out the four stars of the Trapezium clearly.

NGC 1973/75/77

DESCRIPTION: Also in Orion's sword is the star cluster and surrounding nebula called NGC 1973/75/77. These are massive young stars glowing blue hot. The stars light the dust in the nebula around them. **VIEWING TIPS:** This star cluster appears as a tiny point of light at the top of the sword (the end toward the belt).

143

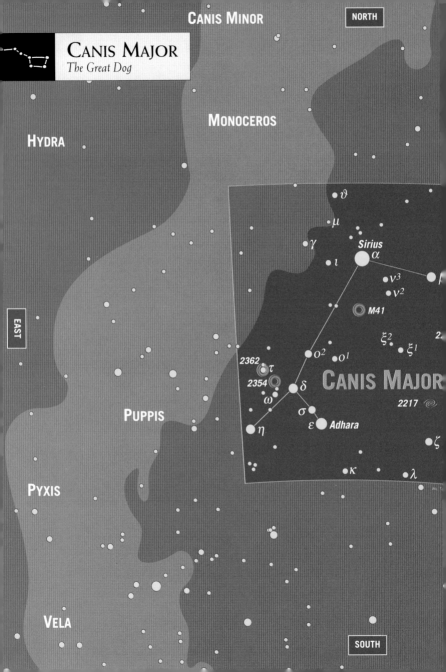

CANIS MINOR

NORTH

CANIS MAJOR
The Great Dog

MONOCEROS

HYDRA

EAST

PUPPIS

PYXIS

VELA

ϑ

μ

γ

Sirius
α

ι

ν³

ν²

M41

ξ²   ξ¹   2.

O²   O¹

2362   τ

2354

ω

δ

CANIS MAJOR

2217

η

σ

ε   Adhara

κ   λ

ζ

SOUTH

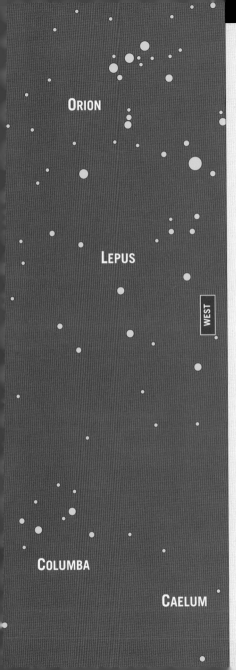

ORION

LEPUS

WEST

COLUMBA

CAELUM

CANIS MAJOR

MYTHOLOGY: Canis Major, the Great Dog, and nearby Canis Minor, the Little Dog, are usually said to be the hunting hounds of Orion.

DESCRIPTION: Canis Major's greatest distinction is its alpha (α) star, Sirius, which is the brightest star in the sky, with a magnitude of -1.5. Sirius and Mirzam (the beta β star) mark the dog's head, and a triangle of stars to the south marks its hindquarters. Another interesting sight in this constellation is the open star cluster M41. Canis Minor, to the north of Canis Major, has only two bright stars, but its alpha (α) star, Procyon, is one of the brightest in the sky.

VIEWING TIPS: Line up Orion's three belt stars and head southeastward. You will pass just above (north of) Sirius. Open star cluster M41 lies south of Sirius. It looks like a single star to the naked eye.

BEST VIEWING TIME: February to March.

SEASON MAPS: Winter.

CANIS MAJOR
Constellation highlights

The large hunting dog companion to Orion features the brightest star in the night sky, Sirius, often called the Dog Star.

DESCRIPTION: Sirius appears so bright in the night sky because of its relative nearness to Earth (it is only 8.8 light-years away) as well as its power output, which is 23 times greater than the sun's output. Sirius is a noticeably bluish-white star. The color is caused by its high temperature, of 17,500°F (9,600°C); it is 1.7 times hotter than the sun. Sirius has a companion star, called Sirius B, a white dwarf star.

VIEWING TIPS: Sirius appears in the southern sky in winter. Through binoculars its blue brilliance is dazzling.

SEASON MAPS: Winter.

SIRIUS B

DESCRIPTION: Sirius B is a white dwarf, a star as massive as most stars, but only about the size of Earth. Sirius B is hotter than its bright companion, Sirius, but it is 10.3 magnitudes (10,000 times) fainter because of its small size. Yet this little star swings its bright companion around with all the gravitational strength of a star the size of the sun. **VIEWING TIPS:** You need a telescope with moderate to high power to bring Sirius B into view, but you will not be able to see it when it is too close to Sirius.

PROCYON (CANIS MINOR)

DESCRIPTION: Not far from Sirius, the Dog Star, is Procyon, the alpha (α) star in the constellation Canis Minor. Procyon's name means "before the dog," and it rises before Sirius in the winter sky. **VIEWING TIPS:** At magnitude 0.4, Procyon is one of the bright stars of the winter sky; it lies to the north, between Sirius and the twin stars of Gemini, Castor and Pollux. It appears on the spring and winter season maps.

147

DESCRIPTION: The Milky Way is a spiral galaxy, but because Earth is positioned in one of the spiral arms in the galaxy's disk, we can't actually see the spiral shape. We see the galaxy from the side, and we can see only stars within our "neighborhood" in the galaxy.

VIEWING TIPS: This map of the Milky Way is drawn from the point of view of a person standing on Earth and watching the night sky over the course of a year. You cannot see all of the Milky Way pictured here at once. In different seasons Earth faces different parts. The center of the map is toward the center of the galaxy. The ends of the map meet one another at a point called the galactic anti-center. The cloudlike areas represent the milky band of the galaxy that we see in the sky. These clouds are stars and nebulas hundreds to thousands of light-years

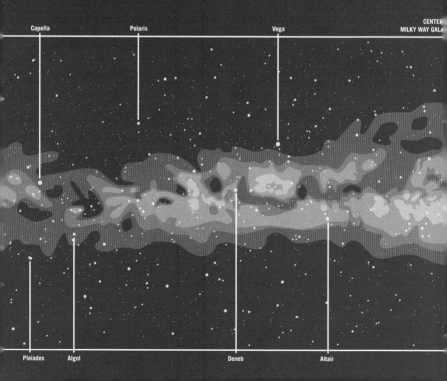

Capella   Polaris   Vega   CENTER MILKY WAY GAL

Pleiades   Algol   Deneb   Altair

away. Many of the night sky's notable stars are labeled, including Capella (constellation Auriga), Algol (Perseus), Polaris (Ursa Minor), Antares (Scorpius), Spica (Virgo), Mimosa and Acrux (Crux, the Southern Cross), Canopus (Carina), Regulus (Leo), Sirius (Canis Major), Procyon (Canis Minor), Betelgeuse and Rigel (Orion), Castor and Pollux (Gemini), and Aldebaran (Taurus). See if you can make out any of the constellations. Look for the stars of the Summer Triangle: Vega (of Lyra),

Deneb (of Cygnus), and Altair (of Aquila) left of the center. The teapot shape of Sagittarius lies just below the center. Rigil Kent and Hadar are bright stars in the constellation Centaurus. Rigil Kent is the third brightest star in the sky, and is the closest star to Earth after the sun—only 4.3 light-years away.

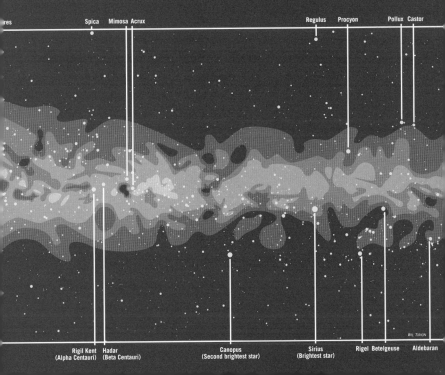

res Spica Mimosa Acrux   Regulus Procyon   Pollux Castor

WIL TIRION

Rigil Kent (Alpha Centauri) Hadar (Beta Centauri)   Canopus (Second brightest star)   Sirius (Brightest star)   Rigel Betelgeuse   Aldebaran

How to use the reference section

The **Glossary,** which begins below, gives definitions of terms used by astronomers. Also in this section are **Solar System Tables** that give dates of the appearances of eclipses, meteor showers, and planets. A listing of **Resources** includes books, software, videos, Web sites, and organizations devoted to astronomy. Finally, there is an **Index** of the topics covered in the book.

Orion Nebula   page 142

GLOSSARY

Alignment
When two or more objects line up with each other.

Asteroid belt
A band between Mars and Jupiter where most asteroids (planetlike chunks of rock) orbit the sun.

Astronomy
The study of everything in space and how it came to be.

Axis
A line through the center of a planet from the north pole to the south pole.

Celestial
Having to do with the sky.

Comet
A body of ice, rock, and gases left over from the formation of our solar system that orbits the sun.

Constellation
A region of the sky, often with a shape formed by connecting stars.

Craters
Dents on the surface of moons or planets created by the impact of crashing rocks.

Degree
A unit of measurement. A circle has 360 degrees.

Diameter
The width of a circular object.

Double star
Two stars close together that often look like one star.

Dwarf
Describes the smallest stars or galaxies.

Eclipse
An event in which one object hides another.

Ecliptic
The plane of the path of Earth's orbit around the sun.

Element
A substance (such as hydrogen or helium) that cannot be broken down into simpler substances.

Elongation
The distance (in degrees) between a planet and the sun from Earth's viewpoint.

Galaxy
A large grouping of stars in space. Galaxies come in different shapes, such as spiral, elliptical, or peculiar.

Gibbous
The moon's shape when it is between half-full and full.

Globular cluster
A ball-shaped grouping of stars.

Gravity
A force that pulls matter toward the center of a star or planet. Earth's gravity makes objects fall to the ground.

Interstellar
Between the stars.

Light-years
A unit of measurement (based on the distance light travels in a year's time) used to calculate huge distances.

Luminous
Giving off light.

Lunar
Having to do with the moon.

Magnetic poles
Northern and southern points of Earth's magnetic field, located near the north and south poles.

Main sequence star
The main period of a star's lifetime, when it generates energy by nuclear fusion.

Magnitude
The measurement of a star's or planet's brightness as seen from Earth.

Meteor
A meteroid (small bit of rock or dust) that falls into Earth's atmosphere and burns up.

Milky Way
The galaxy in which our solar system is located.

Mythology
Legends from ancient civilizations, often with gods and magical creatures.

Nebula
A cloud of gases and dust where stars and planets are born.

Nuclear fusion
One way in which a star generates energy. Occurs in the star's core when four hydrogen atoms fuse into one helium atom, creating energy.

Nucleus
The highly energetic center of a body such as a comet or galaxy.

Open cluster
A loose grouping of stars.

Orbit
A circular or oval path followed by objects in space around another object. In our solar system, the planets orbit the sun, and our moon orbits Earth.

Plane
A flat, level surface. The plane of the solar system or the plane of Earth's orbit can be thought of as flat and round, like a plate.

Planet
A rocky or gaseous body that revolves around a star.

Revolve
To circle around another object. The planets revolve around the sun.

Rotate
To spin.

Satellite
A man-made or natural object (such as a moon) that orbits around another object.

Solar
Having to do with the sun.

Solar system
A star, such as our sun, and the planets and moons that revolve around it.

Solar wind
Energized particles that flow from the sun.

Star
A large ball of hot, shining, electrically charged gases.

Stellar
Having to do with the stars.

Supergiant
Describes the largest stars and galaxies.

Supernova
A star that has exploded at the end of its lifetime.

Universe
Outer space and all the objects in it.

Waning
Growing smaller. The moon wanes after it is full.

Waxing
Growing larger. The moon waxes before it is full.

Zenith
The point directly above an observer's head.

Zodiac
The band of constellations lying in the same plane as the ecliptic.

Neptune page 72

SOLAR SYSTEM TABLES

SOLAR ECLIPSES
June 1999–December 2009

- Dates and times are in Eastern Standard Time (EST). They give the time of mid-eclipse.
- Region is given for around mid-eclipse.
- Type is either total (T), partial (P), or ring (R).

Date	Time	Region	Type
08/11/99	06:03am	Eurasia	T
02/05/00	07:48am	Antarctica	P
07/01/00	02:31pm	S. Pacific/Antarctica	P
07/30/00	09:12pm	Arctic/N. Canada	P
12/25/00	12:34pm	Canada	P
06/21/01	07:03am	S. Atlantic/S. Africa	T
12/14/01	03:51pm	Indonesia/Pacific	R
06/10/02	06:43pm	Central Pacific	R
12/04/02	02:30am	S. Indian Ocean	T
05/30/03	11:07pm	Norwegian Sea/Arctic	R
11/23/03	05:48pm	Antarctica/S. Indian	T
04/19/04	08:33am	S. Atlantic/S. Indian	P
10/13/04	09:58pm	Alaska/Arctic	P
04/08/05	03:35pm	Pacific	R,T
10/03/05	05:30am	Africa	R
03/29/06	05:10am	N. Africa	T
09/22/06	06:39am	Atlantic Ocean	R
03/18/07	09:31pm	Greenland/N. Atlantic	P
09/11/07	07:30am	S.E. Pacific	P
02/06/08	10:54pm	S. Pacific	R
08/01/08	05:20am	Canada	T
01/26/09	02:57am	Indian Ocean	R
07/21/09	09:34pm	E. Pacific	T

LUNAR ECLIPSES
June 1999–December 2009

- Dates and times are in Eastern Standard Time (EST). They give the time of mid-eclipse.
- Type is either total (T) or partial umbra (P).

Date	Time	Type
07/28/99	06:32am	P
01/20/00	11:45pm	T
05/15/03	10:41pm	T
11/08/03	08:18pm	T
10/27/04	10:02pm	T
10/17/05	07:00am	P
08/28/07	05:34am	T
02/20/08	10:26pm	T

PLANET TABLES

The planet tables on the right list the zodiac constellation (abbreviations are listed below) in which each planet can be found at a particular month and year (dates are for the 15th of each month). If a month is not listed, the planet cannot be seen at that time. After looking up which constellation the planet is in, use the seasonal sky maps to find that constellation in the sky.

METEOR SHOWERS

Name	Peak Date	Constellation
Quadrantids	Jan 04	Boötes
Lyrids	Apr 21	Lyra
Eta Aquarids	May 04	Aquarius
Delta Aquarids	Jul 28	Aquarius
Perseids	Aug 12	Perseus
Draconids	Oct 08	Draco
Orionids	Oct 21	Orion
South Taurids	Nov 03	Taurus
Leonids	Nov 16	Leo
Geminids	Dec 13	Gemini

CONSTELLATION ABBREVIATIONS

Name	Abbreviation
Aries	Ari
Pisces	Psc
Aquarius	Aqr
Capricornus	Cap
Sagittarius	Sgr
Ophiuchus	Oph
Scorpius	Sco
Libra	Lib
Virgo	Vir
Leo	Leo
Cancer	Cnc
Gemini	Gem
Taurus	Tau

MERCURY	
Month/Year	Constellation
10/99	Lib/pm
2/00	Aqr/pm
3/00	Aqr/am
4/00	Psc/am
6/00	Gem/pm
3/01	Cap–Aqr/am
5/01	Tau/pm
7/01	Gem/am
2/02	Sgr–Cap/am
3/02	Aqr/am
6/02	Tau/am
12/02	Sgr/pm
2/03	Sgr–Cap/am
4/03	Ari/pm
6/03	Tau/am
12/03	Sgr/pm
1/04	Sgr/am
5/04	Psc/am
7/04	Cnc–Leo/pm
11/04	Sco–Oph/pm
1/05	Sgr/am
3/05	Psc/pm
4/05	Psc/am
5/05	Ari/am
6/05	Gem/pm
7/05	Cnc–Leo/pm
8/05	Cnc/am
12/05	Sco/am
2/06	Aqr/pm
4/06	Psc/am
6/06	Gem/pm
2/07	Aqr/pm
3/07	Cap–Aqr/am
4/07	Psc/am
5/07	Tau/pm
6/07	Gem/pm
7/07	Gem/am
1/08	Cap/pm
2/08	Aqr–Cap/am
3/08	Aqr/am
5/08	Tau/pm
2/09	Cap/am
3/09	Aqr/am
4/09	Ari/pm
6/09	Tau/am
12/09	Sgr/pm

VENUS	
9/99–10/99	Cnc–Leo/am
11/99	Vir/am
12/99	Lib/am
1/00	Oph/am
2/00	Sgr/am
3/00	Aqr/am
4/00	Psc/am
9/00	Vir/pm
10/00	Lib/pm
11/00	Sgr/pm
12/00	Cap/pm
1/01	Aqr/pm
2/01–3/01	Psc/pm
4/01–5/01	Psc/am
6/01	Ari/am
7/01	Tau/am
8/01	Gem/am
9/01–10/01	Leo/am
3/02	Psc/am
4/02	Ari/pm
5/02	Tau/pm
6/02	Cnc/pm
7/02	Leo/pm
8/02–9/02	Vir/pm
10/02	Lib/pm
11/02	Vir/am
12/02	Lib/am
1/03	Sco–Oph/am
2/03	Sgr/am
3/03	Cap/am
4/03	Aqr–Psc/am
5/03	Psc–Ari/am
6/03	Tau/am
11/03	Oph/pm
12/03	Sgr/pm
1/04	Aqr/pm
2/04	Psc/pm
3/04	Ari/pm
4/04–5/04	Tau/am
7/04	Tau/am
8/04	Gem/am
9/04	Cnc/am
10/04	Leo/am
11/04	Vir/am
12/04	Lib/am
1/05	Sgr/am
6/05	Gem/pm
7/05	Leo/pm
8/05–9/05	Vir/pm
10/05	Sco–Oph/pm
11/05	Sgr/pm
12/05	Cap/pm
2/06	Sgr/am
3/06	Cap/am
4/06	Aqr/am
5/06	Psc/am
6/06	Ari/am
7/06	Tau/am
8/06	Cnc/am

1/07	Cap/pm
2/07	Aqr–Psc/pm
3/07	Psc–Ari/pm
4/07	Tau/pm
5/07	Gem/pm
6/07	Cnc/pm
7/07	Leo/pm
9/07	Cnc/am
10/07	Leo/am
11/07	Vir/am
12/07	Lib/am
1/08	Oph/am
2/08	Sgr–Cap/am
3/08	Aqr/am
4/08	Psc/am
9/08	Vir/pm
10/08	Lib/pm
11/08	Sgr/pm
12/08	Cap/pm
1/09	Aqr/pm
2/09–3/09	Psc/pm
4/09–5/09	Psc/am
6/09	Ari/am
7/09	Tau/am
8/09	Gem/am
9/09	Leo/am

MARS	
9/99	Sco–Oph
10/99–11/99	Oph–Sgr
12/99	Cap
1/00	Aqr
2/00–3/00	Psc
4/00	Ari
5/00	Tau
9/00–10/00	Leo
11/00–12/00	Vir
1/01	Lib
2/01	Lib–Sco
3/01–10/01	Oph–Sgr
11/01	Cap
12/01	Aqr
1/02–2/02	Psc
3/02	Ari
4/02–5/02	Tau
6/02	Gem
11/02–12/02	Vir–Lib
1/03	Lib–Sco
2/03	Oph
3/03–5/03	Sgr–Cap
6/03–11/03	Aqr
12/03–1/04	Psc
2/04–4/04	Ari–Tau
5/04–7/04	Gem–Cnc
11/04	Vir

12/04	Lib
1/05	Oph
2/05–4/05	Sgr–Cap
5/05	Aqr
6/05–7/05	Psc
8/05–3/06	Ari-Tau
4/06–5/06	Tau–Gem
6/06	Cnc
7/06–8/06	Leo
12/06	Sco–Oph
1/07–2/07	Oph–Sgr
3/07	Cap
4/07	Aqr
5/07–6/07	Psc
7/07	Ari
8/07–4/08	Tau–Gem
5/08	Cnc
6/08–7/08	Leo
8/08	Vir
2/09–3/09	Cap–Aqr
4/09–5/09	Aqr–Psc
6/09	Ari
7/09–8/09	Tau
9/09–11/09	Gem–Cnc
12/09	Leo

JUPITER	
9/99–1/00	Psc
2/00	Psc–Ari
3/00–4/00	Ari
6/00–5/01	Tau
7/01	Tau–Gem
8/01–6/02	Gem
8/02–10/02	Cnc
11/02–12/02	Cnc–Leo
1/03–6/03	Cnc
7/03–8/04	Leo
11/04–9/05	Vir
12/05–12/06	Lib
1/07–11/07	Oph
1/08–12/08	Sgr
2/09–5/09	Cap
6/09	Cap–Aqr
7/09–12/09	Cap

SATURN	
9/99–4/00	Ari
6/00–5/03	Tau
7/03–6/05	Gem
8/05–7/06	Cnc
9/06–8/09	Leo
10/09–12/09	Vir

RESOURCES

FOR FURTHER READING

The Binocular Stargazer: A Beginner's Guide to Exploring the Sky
Leslie Peltier
Kalmbach Publishing Co., 1995

Black Holes: A Traveler's Guide
Clifford A. Pickover
John Wiley & Sons, 1996

Broca's Brain: Reflections on the Romance of Science
Carl Sagan
Ballantine Books, 1993

Comets: Creators and Destroyers
David Levy
Touchstone Books, 1998

Cosmos
Carl Sagan
Peter Smith Publications, 1988

Discover Planetwatch: A Year Round Viewing Guide to the Night Sky with a Make-Your-Own Planet Finder
Clint Hatchett and Brian Sullivan
Hyperion Books, 1993

Exploring the Moon Through Binoculars and Small Telescopes
Ernest Cherrington
Dover Publications, 1984

A Man on the Moon: The Voyages of the Apollo Astronauts
Andrew Chaikin and Tom Hanks
Penguin USA, 1998

National Audubon Society Field Guide to the Night Sky
Mark R. Chartrand
Alfred A. Knopf, 1995

National Audubon Society Pocket Guides: Constellations, Galaxies and Other Deep-Sky Objects, Planets and Their Moons, The Sun and Moon
Gary Mechler, et al.
Alfred A. Knopf, 1995

1001 Things Everyone Should Know About the Universe
William Gutsch
Doubleday, 1998

Stephen Hawking's Universe: The Cosmos Explained
David Filkin and Stephen Hawking
Basic Books, 1998

365 Starry Nights: An Introduction to Astronomy for Every Night of the Year
Chet Raymo
Simon & Schuster, 1992

The 21st Century in Space
(Isaac Asimov's New Library of the Universe)
Isaac Asimov, et al.
Gareth Stevens, 1996

A Walk through the Heavens
Milton D Heifetz and Wil Tirion
Cambridge Univ. Press, 1996

Whitney's Star Finder
Charles A. Whitney
Alfred A. Knopf, 1989

SOFTWARE

Astro 2001: The Wonders of the Universe
Zdenek Pokorny, et al.
Andromeda Software, Inc.

Astronomy Star Finder for Windows
Franz Hack
Abacus Software, 1993

Beyond Planet Earth
The Discovery Channel
Multimedia 2000, 1995

Eyewitness Encyclopedia of Space and the Universe
DK Book Co., 1997

The History of the Universe
Ransom Publishing, 1997

Mars: Past, Present, and Future
Holiday Interactive, 1998

Redshift 3
Maris Multimedia
Piranha Interactive Publishing, Inc., 1998

Scientific American: Planets
Simon & Schuster, 1995

Scientific American: The Universe: From Quarks to Cosmos
Simon & Schuster, 1997

Solar System Explorer
Maris Multimedia
Daval Publications, 1997

VIDEOS

Apollo 13
MCA/Universal Home Video, 1995

Asteroids: Deadly Impact
National Geographic Video, 1997

The Astronomers
PBS Home Video
Tel: 800-222-5795

Astronomy 101: A Beginner's Guide to the Night Sky
Mazon Productions, 1994

Cosmos
Carl Sagan
Turner Home
Entertainment, 1979

The Creation of the Universe
Timothy Ferris
PBS Home Video, 1985

Death of a Star
What Einstein Never Knew
Kidnapped by UFOs?
Venus Unveiled
NOVA programs
Tel: 800-255-9424

From the Earth to the Moon
HBO Studios, 1998

IMAX's The Dream is Alive (1995), Destiny in Space (1994), Blue Planet (1990)
Tel: 800-263-IMAX

The Miracle Planet: The Third Planet
Ambrose Video Publishing
Tel: 800-843-0048

Mysteries of Deep Space
PBS Home Video

The Really Big World of Astronomy
The Standard Deviants
Cerebellum Corporation
Tel: 800-VCR-REVU
http://www.cerebellum.com

Space Age
Public Media Video
Tel: 800-262-8600

Stephen Hawking's Universe
PBS Home Video, 1997

ORGANIZATIONS & WEB SITES

Andromeda Software, Inc.
http://www.andromedasoftware.com

Asteroid and Comet Impact Hazards
http://impact.arc.nasa.gov/index.html

Astrobiology
http://astrobiology.arc.nasa.gov/home.html

The Astronaut Connection
http://nauts.com

Astronomical Society of the Pacific
Tel: 415-337-1100
http://www.aspsky.org

Auroras: Paintings in the Sky
http://www.exploratorium.edu/learning_studio/auroras

Bradford Robotic Telescope
http://www.eia.brad.ac.uk/btl

EarthWatch International
680 Mount Auburn Street
P.O. Box 403
Watertown, MA 02272
Tel: 800-776-0188
http://www.earthwatch.org

Griffith Observatory
http://www.griffithobs.org

GSOC Satellite Predictions
http://www.gsoc.dlr.de/satvis

Hale-Bopp
http://www.sipe.com/halebopp/tocmap.htm

Int'l Dark Sky Association
http://www.darksky.org

Liftoff to Space Exploration
http://liftoff.msfc.nasa.gov

MWO Online StarMap
http://www.mtwilson.edu/Services/StarMap

NASA Spacelink
http://spacelink.msfc.nasa.gov

National Audubon Society
700 Broadway
New York, NY 10003-9562
Tel: 212-979-3000
http://www.audubon.org

National Space Society
http://www.nss.org

Observatorio Arval: Moon Map
http://www.arval.org.ve/MoonMapen.htm

Piranha Interactive Marketing
Tel: 602-491-0500
http://www.piranhainteractive.com

The Planetary Society
http://planetary.org

Sky Publishing Corporation
Tel: 800-253-0245
http://www.skypub.com

Space Telescope Science Institute Home Page
http://www.stsci.edu

Students for the Exploration and Development of Space
http://seds.lpl.arizona.edu

Willmann-Bell, Inc.
Tel: 804- 320-7016
http://www.willbell.com

Zephyr Services
Tel: 412-422-6600
http://www.zephyrs.com

INDEX

The moon, Jupiter, and Venus

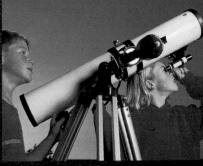

PHOTO CREDITS

Credits are listed by page, from left to right, top to bottom.

Front Cover: Jerry Schad/Science Source/Photo Researchers, Inc.
Half-title page (Saturn): NASA/Astrostock*Sanford
Title Page (Horsehead Nebula): Tony & Daphne Hallas/Astro Photo
Table of Contents (solar eclipse): Frank Zullo/Photo Researchers, Inc.
6: Anglo-Australian Observatory
8a: Courtesy of The Maria Mitchell Association
8b: Lior Rubin
9a: Jessica Wecker/Photo Researchers, Inc.
9b: Z. Carter
9c: Jessica Wecker/Photo Researchers, Inc.
10–11: Chris Butler/Photo Researchers, Inc.
11a: T. Boroson/National Optical Astronomy Observatories
12–13: National Optical Astronomy Observatories
13a: Science Photo Library/Photo Researchers, Inc.
13b: NASA/JSC/STScI
15: NASA/STScI
16–17 (background): David Malin/Anglo-Australian Observatory
16a: David Malin/Anglo-Australian Observatory
16b: T. Boroson/National Optical Astronomy Observatories
17: David Malin/Anglo-Australian Observatory

20–21 (background): NOAO/Phil Degginger/Color-Pic, Inc.
20a: NASA
20b: John Sanford/Astrostock*Sanford
23: David Malin/Anglo-Australian Observatory
24a: John Sanford and David Parker/Science Photo Library/Photo Researchers, Inc.
24b: John Sanford and David Parker/Science Photo Library/Photo Researchers, Inc.
30: NASA
32 (Earth): NASA
33a: Lick Observatory
33b: NASA
34a: John Sanford/Astrostock*Sanford
34b: Patrick A. Wiggins/Hansen Planetarium/University of Utah
35: E. R. Degginger/Color-Pic, Inc.
36–37 (background): Lee C. Coombs
38–39 (background): Lee C. Coombs
39a (Mars): John Sanford/Astrostock*Sanford
39b (Saturn): Lee C. Coombs
39c (Jupiter): Michael A. Covington
41: NASA/JPL/Caltech
44: Anglo-Australian Observatory
46: John Sanford/Astrostock*Sanford
48: Luke Dodd/Science Photo Library/Photo Researchers, Inc.
50: Lee C. Coombs

51a: John Sanford/Astrostock*Sanford
51b: National Optical Astronomy Observatories/NSO, Sacramento Peak
52: Warren Faidley/Weatherstock
53a: NOAO/Phil Degginger/Color-Pic, Inc.
53b: NOAO/Phil Degginger/Color-Pic, Inc.
54: James H. Robinson/Photo Researchers, Inc.
55a: John Bova/Photo Researchers, Inc.
55b: John Sanford/Astrostock*Sanford
58: William H. Mullins/Photo Researchers, Inc.
59a: Akira Fujii
59b: Michael A. Covington
60: Jerry Schad/Photo Researchers, Inc.
61a: Space Imagery Center, Lunar & Planetary Lab, University of Arizona
61b: Phil Degginger/Color-Pic, Inc.
62: John Sanford/Astrostock*Sanford
63a: NASA/Phil Degginger/Color-Pic, Inc.
63b: NASA/JPL/Caltech
64: John Sanford/Astrostock*Sanford
65a: Dr. Robert Leighton/JPL/Astrostock*Sanford
65b: NASA/JPL/Caltech
66: Jerry Schad/Photo Researchers, Inc.
67a: NASA/Astronomical Society of the Pacific
67b: NASA/Astronomical

Prepared and produced by
Chanticleer Press, Inc.

Publisher: Andrew Stewart
Founder: Paul Steiner

Chanticleer Staff:
Editor-in-Chief: Amy K. Hughes
Senior Editor: Miriam Harris
Managing Editor: George Scott
Associate Editor: Michelle Bredeson
Assistant Editor: Elizabeth Wright
Editorial Assistants: Amy Oh, Anne O'Connor
Photo Director: Zan Carter
Photo Editors: Ruth Jeyaveeran, Jennifer McClanaghan
Assistant Photo Editor: Meg Kuhta
Rights and Permissions Manager: Alyssa Sachar
Photo Assistants: Leslie Fink, Karin Murphy
Art Director: Drew Stevens
Designers: Kirsten Berger, Brian Boyce, Anthony Liptak,
Vincent Mejia, Bernadette Vibar
Director of Production: Alicia Mills
Production Manager: Philip Pfeifer

Contributors:
Writer: Gary Mechler
Consultant: Amie Gallagher
Sky maps: Wil Tirion
Illustrations: Howard S. Friedman
Icons: Holly Kowitt

Scholastic Inc. Staff:
Editorial Director: Wendy Barish, Creative Director: David Saylor,
Managing Editor: Manuela Soares, Manufacturing Manager: Karen Fuchs

Original Series Design: Chic Simple Design